PROBLEMS IN EDUCATION

JONAS F. SOLTIS
Professor of Philosophy and Education
Teachers College, Columbia University

and

JONATHAN C. MESSERLI
Dean, School of Education
Hofstra University,

Co-Editors

In every age educators not only face new problems unique to their times, but also redefine many old problems in light of present conditions. This series is intended to provide anthologies containing comprehensive sets of readings which directly address themselves to some single major contemporary issue in educational scholarship, theory, or practice. The purpose of the series is not merely to inform students and educators about important contemporary problems, but to inform their **thinking** about these problems so that they may deal with them more wisely and effectively.

Aims of Education

edited by

LESLIE M. BROWN

TEACHERS COLLEGE PRESS
Teachers College, Columbia University
NEW YORK, NEW YORK

Preface

There seems never to be a time when educators are free from questions or problems relating to their aims in educating, for most societies view formal education as a vehicle for arriving at some worthwhile destination or as an instrument to be used to shape some desirable end product. But especially today, when the very world in which we live is threatened with destruction, and when the fundamental values and purposes of human forms of association are under serious question, and most especially when formal education itself is squarely faced with the charge of being irrelevant to the lives of those whom it purports to educate, a full scale reassessment of the aims of education by educators and critics of education alike seems to be inevitable.

Thus, this anthology is timely; but more than that, it provides an organized way to intelligently examine the many types of aims which have been or yet may be advanced seriously as the proper ends for educating. It also shows quite directly that deciding wisely about desirable directions for education is indeed a complex business. For those who would face conscientiously the major contemporary problems surrounding the question of valid and valuable educational aims, this volume presents the multiple dimensions of those problems in straightforward terms and supplies some of the best thoughts on the subject from Plato to the present. No single answer to what we should aim at is advocated, but the basis for thinking intelligently about this central educational issue in today's complex world is put within the reach of the thoughtful reader.

Jonas F. Soltis
Teachers College
Columbia University

Contents

PART III   Personal Ends-In-View

PART IV   The Nature of Aims in Education

General Introduction

It is sometimes said that education is in the public domain, but what is open to public discussion, such as the purposes of education, is not necessarily publicly held. Every public question is liable to be viewed from many personal standpoints. It is just as likely to be influenced by prejudice and short-sightedness as by impartiality and perceptiveness. What is evident in all public discussions is not so much a merging of viewpoints as a personal slant on things—whether the topic be presidential elections, racism, or the purposes of education. Few of us seem readily able to change the lenses through we see the world, however "public" may be the forum from which we speak. Even objectivity is an expression of individuality; it is one of a man's recognizable dispositions.

In the sense, therefore, that most people nowadays have opinions about education, it is certainly a subject that is in the public domain, though the various opinions are influenced by each individual's accumulated experiences, personality, and circumstances. Perhaps for that reason, more than for any other, expressions of opinion by laymen about the general aim of education are apt to be as divergent as: 1. to learn a useful trade, 2. to make life interesting and enjoyable, 3. to get basic knowledge and skills for everyday living, 4. to become independent of parents or guardians, and 5. to learn a worthwhile vocation.

Whereas personal factors seem to provide one impulse for airing views about what education should be aiming at, or what its purpose should be, another such impulse seems to spring from commitment to cultural values. This would appear to be the case when general aims such as: 1. to contribute to an informed citizenship, 2. to create a society based on values of cooperation and sharing, 3. to make for perfect social efficiency, 4. to create a perfectly stable world order, and 5. to lead to a brotherhood of mankind are formulated.

Juxtaposing these two sets of aims, one will observe that the former are more "individual oriented." Aims such as these one may call *private* or *self-aims*. They are concerned with satisfying personal needs—such as improved self-mastery and acceptance by others—and desires—such as a vocation and independent means of support. The second set of aims is "public oriented." Aims such as these one may call *public aims*. These demonstrate a consideration of the interests of others, or of society or humanity as a whole. Legislating for mankind, the authors of these aims may prescribe them for reasons of greater happiness, a stronger moral sense, a reduction of narrow individualism, and so forth.

One will observe that educational aims form two groups in another way: Some aims are potentially *attainable,* others unattainable. There is little room for doubt that for most people the learning of a useful trade is an attainable aim. There is much room for doubt, though, about the attainability of an aim such as "to create a perfectly stable world order which will lead to a brotherhood of mankind." Whereas some aims refer to practicable achievement in the everyday world, then, others refer rather to ideals which by their nature are visionary and beyond realization in the everyday world.

In a sense the most public of all aims are those that are not personally held, but are shared as the identifiable paraphernalia of educational theory. They may be piled up as a bleached accumulation of possibilities in a lecture or an education seminar and turned over and over in academic discussion until the words are polished and the differences apparently reconciled. But once abstracted from experience and made impersonal in this way they are strictly not aims at all, but aim-skeletons. As such, they belong to no one personally: they are public property, like the objects of a national museum. Thus objectified, such aims are also inert.

Although private aims, by definition, cannot be characterized in this way, public aims are by their very nature suspect in this respect, for there is something logically odd in proposing an aim for others to experience. What is the function of external aim-makers—those who undertake to prescribe aims for others to experience? Is there not a suspicion that some will be merely constructing and manipulating life-less aim-models? Apart from this factitious impulse, who among the external aim-makers can claim the power to successfully implant his own living aim into another's mind? There are two unwarranted assumptions here: the first is the practicability of knowing another's mind sufficiently well to justify a belief that the aim will be psychologically assimilable, or that it will "take"; the second is that an individual will choose what another wants him to choose. It is the choice-gap, in particular, that tends to be overlooked in the logic of aim-prescribing.

Perhaps there is some reason to expect that the vaguest of aims will be those propounded by a particular section of external aim-makers, those not speaking with the clarity of personal conviction or private directiveness, but rather indulging a propensity for reformist theorizing. Then there may appear such unexplained ends of education as "self-fulfilment," or "social progress." But two other sources of vagueness in aim statements are concerned with a failure to analyze concepts. First, it is frequently found that whatever is predicated on aims calls for further analysis, so that a statement of a general aim of education raises a number of other questions. In such situations the heart of the problem is to be reached only by peeling off layer after layer of deceptively simple and promising surfaces. Aristotle found the existing practice of Athenian education perplexing partly because it was not clear to him "whether education is more concerned with intellectual or with moral virtue." But even if Athenians had all agreed that education should aim primarily at virtue, the clarity of aims could have been attained only by first reaching agreement on the nature of virtue, and on this, as Aristotle acknowledged, people have "different ideas."[1] The second source of conceptual vagueness is the word "aim" itself. One of the reasons for this is that aim-language is apt to be used as a vehicle for persuasive intentions. Indeed, in many educational discussions "aim" and its cognates have become prestige words. It is sometimes argued that nothing can be more negative or ineffectual than to proceed on a course without aim or purpose. Aimless behavior is held to be characteristic of the unintelligent. Conversely, it is usually held that to be intelli-

[1] Jowett, B. (trans.): *The Politics of Aristotle,* Oxford: Clarendon Press, 1855, p. 245.

gent is not merely to *have* an aim, but to aim clearly *at something.* Aiming is thus identified with *taking aim,* with focusing positively and purposefully on a perceived end-in-view. And the most vital step of all in intelligent behavior is held to be decisive action toward the realization of the desired end-in-view.

It is an easy transition from this general aim-theorizing to perceive an unwarranted aura of efficacy about aims of any kind, and from this halo-effect to fail to recognize the vagueness that is sometimes associated with it. Such occasional vagueness is aggravated by a tendency for some to use aim words loosely, if not interchangeably. To assist in clarifying these words in ordinary language, we will use the term "end-in-view"[2] to include "ideal," "objective," and "goal," and will make an introductory analysis of these three members of the aim-family.

One commonly used definition of the term "ideal" describes it as an end-in-view that is both perfect and unattainable. Although some cherish such ideals and are fully aware of their unattainability, there are others who condemn them as vague and verbalistic, declaring them unrelated to human conduct. This first sense of ideal may be illustrated by the ideal of the perfect state or society which many dream of but which none achieve. But there is a second sense of the term which is directed at partial attainability rather than at perfectibility. Here there is a much stronger appreciation of the potential motivating power of the ideal, a feeling that the ideal can guide and modify behavior. One may speak, in this sense, of educating *toward* an ideal of racial tolerance, or *toward* an ideal of humanitarianism. Although remoteness and unattainability are common to both senses, ideals are not on that account to be relegated to a world of dreams or fantasies. Recognition of the second sense, in particular, enables one to see that ideals have a legitimate place in the observable world of everyday deeds, where as motivating symbols they often give impetus and direction to behavior.

In common usage "objective" tends to contrast with "ideal." Whereas ideals are generally unattainable, objectives are generally attainable. Objectives may be simple and short-range—like the memorization of a lyric—or complex and long-range—like the development of tolerance toward other people—but they are essentially realizable. It

[2] This term was limited by Dewey to cases where consequences could be foreseen. John Dewey, *Theory of Valuation,* Chicago: University of Chicago Press, 1939, p. 25ff.

is exceptional to speak of remote objectives in education, and it is usually contradictory to speak of unachievable ones.

The term "goal" appears to occupy an intermediate position between ideal and objective. In each of the two senses in which ideal has been discussed there is an intersection with goal. One may refer in the first sense to an end-in-view that is dream-like, visionary, or so remote and unattainable as to engage few to personal commitment: "The ultimate goal of education is the moral unification of all mankind." Or one may speak, with a more realistic appreciation of what is practicable, of educators striving toward a goal of complete world literacy, while still acknowledging the probability that achievement will fall short of the goal in the foreseeable future. The more frequent use of "goal," however, is as an end-in-view that is at least logically attainable in the sense that in declaring it attainable one is not contravening laws of reason. It is sometimes said that students should have academic goals which are realistic levels of aspiration, and which match their respective abilities. In this case, "goal" retains a motivational power, and is perceived as a condition or state of affairs toward which behavior is directed. It is common in educational psychology to attribute to goals qualities of directiveness and attainability, and there is a pronounced tendency to use the term for *private* ends-in-view, and "objective" for *public* ends-in-view. Teachers and examiners have educational objectives for students; individual students and teachers have goals for themselves.

The common usage distinctions that have been drawn among ends-in-view or aims may now be represented diagrammatically, with the reservation that considerable looseness and interchangeability still prevail among all members of this word family. The system of classification in Figure 1 (see p. xiv) is based on the criterion of *attainability*. It would be an oversimplification to represent ideals and objectives as mutually exclusive, although they are almost so. Whereas ultimately objectives are attainable and ideals are not, some ideals do become objectives to the extent that they become partially attained.

By a second convenient criterion for classifying ends-in-view—namely, that of *orientation*—one is able to distinguish between private and public ends-in-view. Since one of the tendencies in both psychological and common usage is for "goal" to be limited to ends-in-view that are private, this distinction will be observed consistently to enable ends-in-view to be classified as either private or public.

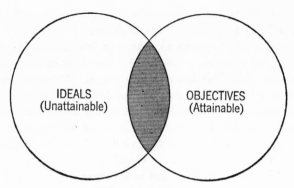

Figure 1. Ends-in-view or aims.

The system of classification in Figure 2 (below) is based on the criterion of orientation. Again, it would be an oversimplification to represent the private and the public as mutually exclusive, although the area of overlap between them is perhaps relatively small. The shaded portion of the figure indicates that some individuals holding private aims may express similar aims for others; likewise, some formulating public aims may be committed to them privately as well. Moreover, the very process of *assimilation* of aims implies that a public aim may sometimes overlap into the private domain. A teacher's aim is public when he attempts to develop in his pupils a sensitivity to social injustice.

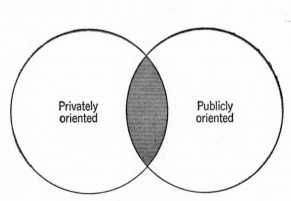

Figure 2. Ends-in-view (ideals and objectives).

It is concurrently a private aim when an individual student becomes committed to it.

Indeed, sensitivity to social injustice falls in the common ground of Figure 2, because in no instance can this objective be realized by pupils *until* it becomes individually assimilated. The reason lies in the complex nature of the objective, compounded of both cognitive and affective elements. It is the *affective* element—with an attitudinal or dispositional dimension — which prevents the full realization of the objective until it has become self-oriented. To develop a sensitivity to social injustice is to do more than impart an *understanding* of a social phenomenon: it is to lead a pupil to the stage where he accepts the feelings involved and assimilates them into his outlook. Similarly, an objective of religious tolerance cannot be attained by pupils while it is viewed by them only as a teacher-expectation. They may be able to grasp the *concept* of religious tolerance, even while the objective remains public. But the *will* to be tolerant involves an independent acceptance of certain feelings and their assimilation into the private world of the learner. The affective element in complex objectives is also evident in educational aims of an aesthetic kind, such as "to develop in pupils a love of group singing," or "to give pupils the satisfaction of creating pleasing designs." Every affective component of a complex objective involves an act of choice, an individual acceptance of a private point of view. As such, the learner's feelings toward the object tend to be lasting rather than ephemeral, and tend to acquire some of the characteristics of an attitude.

There are certain objectives with both cognitive and affective elements which fall between the simple and the complex. For instance, a lyrical poem may have a spontaneous appeal. The teacher's presentation may be such that the objective is a combined teacher-pupil one, the distinction between public and private objectives disappearing. In such a case, the pupils will begin the experience either with open attitudes toward poetry or toward the teacher, or with decisively favorable ones. Both directness and speed of realization would mark such an objective as a simple one. However, if in another instance pupil attitudes happen to be favorable toward poetry and unfavorable toward the teacher, that teacher's objective might well be a complex one, involving slow attitude modification.

In this anthology the complex objective will not be characterized merely by the presence of both cognitive and affective elements, but by the union of these where the affective element is also of an attitudinal or *dispositional* kind.

The distinction between the public formulation and the private acceptance of complex objectives, and the significance of the affective element in them, becomes evident when one recognizes the limitations of the teacher's power to literally "give" or "impart" any educational objective. Where feelings are concerned, he can do no more than lead his pupils to water. He can teach unwilling pupils that 6 x 6 = 36, and to apathetic ones he can impart an understanding of abstract principles. But he cannot himself literally *give* anyone feelings, for example, for conservation, love of good music, or commitment to democratic ideals. In each of these instances, beyond the facts and the comprehension of principles or concepts, there is a door to the pupil's feelings which only the pupil can open.

Several propositions may be stated in review to indicate the main types of ends-in-view to be illustrated and examined in the pages which follow:

a. Some ends-in-view are attainable, some are not.

b. Some ends-in-view are relatively easy and quick to attain (short-range), others are relatively difficult and slow to attain (long-range).

c. Some ends-in-view are simple, others are complex.

d. Some ends-in-view are public, others are private.

With these distinctions in mind, ends-in-view may be classified and juxtaposed in two ways according to the two main sets of criteria: first, on attainability and degree of simplicity; second, on intended orientation—whether the end-in-view is for oneself to pursue, or for others to pursue. The four classes of ends-in-view are:

I. Class R: A class of *remote* ends-in-view, or ideals. These are characterized by unattainability, though some are partially attainable.

II. Class S: A contrasting class of *simple* ends-in-view or short-range objectives. These are characterized by ready attainability.

III. Class C: A class of *complex* dispositional ends-in-view or long-range objectives, composed of both cognitive and affective elements. They are characterized by complexity and relative slowness and difficulty of attainment, in each respect contrasting with the simple, short-range objectives in Class S.

IV. Class P: A class of *private* ends-in-view or goals composed of all ideals and objectives which are oriented toward the self. They may have been self-initiated, or they may have been completely assimilated from others' formulations. In either case, they are private, contrasting with all those in preceding classes which are intended for others.

The terminology to be adopted in this anthology may now be summarized, though individual selections will, of course, retain their respective authors' terminology:

End-in-view: the generic name, including within it "ideal" and "objective."

Goal: If the "ideal" or "objective" is private, it may be referred to as a "goal." As such it is both motivating and directive.

Ideal: Ideals are unattainable, remote, potentially directive.

Objective: Objectives are attainable and potentially directive. They may be subdivided into simple objectives, which are relatively quick and easy to attain, and complex objectives, which are relatively difficult to attain.

Aim: Aim is a generic name used as an alternative to "ends-in-view." [3]

The classifications have already indicated the main conceptual features to be recognized throughout this study of aims, but their relative dispositions require explanation. As far as possible, an antithetical principle is employed both between chapters and within them. Thus, ideals in Chapters 1 and 2 are opposed to simple objectives in Chapter 3; the complex objectives in Chapter 4 contrast also with the simple objectives of Chapter 3; and the complex objectives of Chapter 4 merge into the private aims of Chapter 5. For although a complex objective may originate externally as a public aim, it has been seen that to be fulfilled it must be assimilated into the learner's private world.

No introduction to aims of education would be complete without emphasizing the many fluid relationships that exist among them. An-

---

[3] The term "aim" is retained in order to avoid pedantry in some contexts and obvious clashes with the terminology of some of the selections.

other aspect of the same emphasis is that the classifications used are for convenience in understanding conceptual relationships: they are not to be regarded as absolute, serving all possible purposes, or indicating hard and fast distinctions in current usage. Some of the possible relationships may now be summarized by reference to the following diagrammatic representation (figure 3).

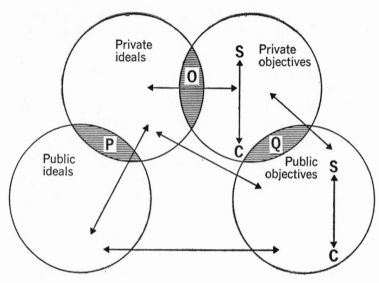

Figure 3.

The shaded area *O* indicates that some private ideals merge into private objectives in so far as they have partial attainability. It also indicates that an individual may concurrently have a private ideal and various private objectives ultimately directed toward it. The shaded area *P* indicates that an individual may have a private ideal that he formulates for others, making it concurrently a public ideal as well. Similarly, the shaded area *Q* indicates that a private objective may concurrently be made public. Arrows from *S* to *C* indicate two-way relationships within classes of objectives, these being from simple to complex and vice-versa. An individual may have a simple private objective that leads to a complex one or, conversely, he may have a complex objective

that leads him to set simpler ones for himself. Similarly, a person holding simple public objectives may proceed to formulate complex public
objectives from them and vice versa. Arrows between classes indicate
possible two-way lines of transition from one class to another. For
instance, an individual may have a private ideal that leads him to set
himself private objectives. He may have a private ideal that leads to
his formulating a public ideal. Private objectives that he holds may
lead him to formulate public objectives. He may have private ideals
that lead him to formulate public objectives, or public ideals that lead
to his formulating public objectives, or even private objectives that lead
to his formulating public ideals. In every instance, the line of transition is reversible between one class and another.

Each line of transition between classes may be duplicated with
imaginary two-way arrows to indicate the transference of aims from
one individual to another, as from teacher to pupil, or from educationist to teacher. To illustrate, a teacher may have a private ideal
which *leads to* a pupil's setting of private objectives. Clearly, the reversibility of this relationship is sometimes doubtful—dependent, as it
always must be, on the different persons at the two ends of the process
—for now there are *two* minds involved. Thus, it would be difficult to
conceive of a pupil's private objectives leading to a teacher's private
ideal, although such a relationship would be theoretically possible. Similarly, it is much more likely that a teacher's publicly formulated ideal
for all his pupils should lead to a pupil's development of a private ideal,
than that a pupil's private ideal should lead to a teacher's formulation
of a public ideal for all his pupils. Such questions of probability are not
strictly relevant to the present purpose, however, *which is to show that
the aim relationships between classes may apply not only to the case
of individual aim-making, but also to the case of transmission of aims
from one person to another,* a transmission that is subject to certain psychological conditions governing interpersonal compatibility.

Further opportunities for studying relationships will emerge in
the following chapters. The final signposts to be set up at this stage are
intended to point to the main organizational divisions of the book.
Part I and Part II are concerned with *public* aims. Part III deals with
contrasting *private* aims. Part IV reflects on the structure, purpose, and
effectiveness of the features observed, and is divided into two sections:
the theoretical viewpoints of others on the aims of education, and tentative conclusions.

Part

I

Ideals

1

Ideals of Citizenship and Society

INTRODUCTION

While to some people ideals are merely the stuff of dreams signifying no more than escapist fantasies, to others they provide the impulse for constantly focusing on some of the conspicuous imperfections of human life. Thus imbued with a reformist zeal, and aiming at something he believed was capable of improving the quality of men's lives, Socrates went about Athens demonstrating how beliefs and opinions should always be held up to the light of reason. His method was to speak with as many individual Athenians as possible, doing each "the greatest of services" (as Plato has him attest in *The Apology*) by discussing virtue and other matters relating to the kind of good life that might be lived by following reason.

Not all educational ideals have such a practical bent as this ideal of Socrates. Although arising also from a sympathetic discontent with the observed conditions of life, some ideals are much more remote and much less closely involved with the practicalities of living. These ideals may be described as broadly inclusive plans for such things as a better social order. But such dreams of visionaries and the speculations of zealous theory-builders are always vulnerable to Socratic questions: What do your words *mean?* How do you know that what you say is *true?* Thus, it is sometimes shown that the vision of a remote ideal lacks substantial foundation in reason or experience—even though it may retain for some people the symbolic motivating gleam of perfection.

In this chapter the general topic to be discussed is educational ends-

1

in-view that are related to an ideal citizenship in an ideal society. Three interrelated themes are taken from *The Republic:*

1. The relation of the individual to the State.
2. Recognition of individual differences among citizens.
3. Education as the basis of the social order.

Ideas are played against each other by having Plato speak first on each theme, then introducing to the rostrum two modern philosophers —Dewey and Nunn—to speak with the advantage of experience from the intervening millennia.

It is understandable that the first of these themes should also have been the first theme of recorded educational theory. It may have been, indeed, even the first educational topic ever discussed, for once individual men became aware that the power of the State was increasing, it is a reasonable speculation that they began to question its authority and to assert the rights of the individual.[1] By the time Plato wrote *The Republic,* however, the pendulum had swung to an excessive individualism, and it was to this that Plato reacted, perhaps with equal excess, by proposing an ideal state characterized by unity and harmony. How could this end be achieved? By loyalty, obedience, and a proper identification, Plato suggests in a selection that follows, everyone knowing his place, whether ruler or ruled, would willingly subordinate himself to the State. This kind of subordination would be neither suppressive nor irksome, for every individual would think of himself as an integral part of the state, as arms and legs are integral parts of the body. Indeed, has not the perfect state a community of feeling, Plato asks, with every member sharing its pleasures and pains, just as all parts of an individual's "body and soul" seem to share the pleasures and pains that have their source in a particular part?

Nunn questions this complete subordination of the individual to the state in the Platonic scheme of things. While conceding that the individual matures in a social environment, he argues that the primary end-in-view for education is not a better society, but better individuals. Nunn thus reverses the coin whose side Plato has earlier displayed. True, society's traditions and institutions are often more lasting than single individuals, but for Nunn these have significance only in so far as they serve individual development. Indeed, education is worthy of the name,

[1] J. Adams, *The Evolution of Educational Theory.* London: Macmillan, 1912, pp. 134-135.

not—as Plato believes—when it "makes a man eagerly pursue the ideal perfection of citizenship, and teaches him how rightly to rule and how to obey,"[2] but when it promotes the full potentialities of individual excellence. For Nunn, the picture of the state as a kind of "super-personal entity" is false. All the energies of education should be bent toward making an interestingly variegated society of *different* individuals, each fully developed according to his unique nature. And the individual is to be free to develop in his own way—even if the way be "cloistral and secluded"—never obliged to be merely a state cipher who denies himself the privacy of his own emotions. In short, Nunn's reply to Plato is that it is the making of free individuals, not the making of the state, that is the worthier educational end-in-view.

Plato now returns to speak on the second theme, that of individual differences among citizens. Every State begins as a community of "partners and helpers," each doing what he is best fitted to do. Hence, a natural division of labor produces farmers, builders, weavers, shoemakers, carpenters, smiths, merchants, shopkeepers, etc., but all of these money-makers fall into one class. The two other classes are those of soldiers (auxiliaries) and rulers (philosophers).

Although the soul may be said to have, like the state itself, three parts—appetite, courage, and reason—in money-makers it is the first of these that is dominant, in soldiers it is the second, and in rulers and rulers only, it is the third. And because it is the rulers only who have been trained as philosophers, they alone have insight into truth. The strength and integrity of the just and perfect state depend on the accurate placing of its members into one of these three classes, with those of each class confining themselves strictly to the work for which nature has best fitted them. Every man must know his stratum and stay there for his own best interests and for the good of all. Only then will there be a perfect equilibrium and a perfectly functioning society.

The antagonist at this point is Dewey, whose remarks have relevance to the first theme as well as to the second. He too has a vision of an ideal society, but perfection and the limits of attainability are kept distinct. He objects, with Plato probably in mind, to setting up ideals "out of our heads," rather than basing them on experience of actual societies. (Here Plato was at a disadvantage, since few societies were

[2] *Laws,* translated by B. Jowett, 4th edition, Oxford: Clarendon Press, 1953, vol. IV, pp. 209-210.

known to him.) Dewey confronts Plato on several counts. First, he argues that individual differences are perceived too coarsely by Plato, with his bundling of all men into one of three groups: to individual uniqueness Plato appears blind. Second, he feels that Plato's ideals are static: individuals are taken to be unchanging and the state, once established, becomes stable, fixed, and eternal. Third, he maintains that Plato's naive dream of a cohesive and unified state in which individuals keep to their classes, play out their narrow roles, and never meddle in others' business, bears no relationship to actual experience. Dewey sees society as pluralistic, with disagreement and diversity as a corollary of freedom.

Dewey's own democratic ideal features a wide sharing of common interests—not merely the Platonic sharing of community feeling—as well as unlimited free interaction among groups. Both principles are alien to Plato's system since they cut across all artificial class boundaries. Moreover, Dewey believes that wider recognition of mutual interests will in itself give a measure of social control. In his system are more trust, less imposition, less apprehension of possible disorder, and an absence of occupational immobilization and of intellectual stagnation among whole classes of people.

Plato returns to deal with his third theme of education as the basis of the social order, by which he means that the state is to be stabilized and even perpetuated by education—particularly by the education of the guardians. At the age of fifty the most distinguished of the guardians will have reached, by education of the proper sort, a state of personal balance, completely content with their lot, seeking nothing in private ownership, rewarded by their capacity to glimpse reality and to live the life of wisdom and insight. And once established in their offices as philosopher-rulers they will educate others as they were educated, so that the state will develop a lasting and indestructible order.

In his educational scheme for guardians, Plato searches for appropriate studies that "will draw the soul away from becoming to being,"[3] away, that is, from knowledge that is merely passing or perishable to the truth of a knowledge that is fixed and immutable. Dialectics

---

[3]*The Republic,* translated by A. D. Lindsay, Everyman's Library. London: J. M. Dent & Sons, 1935, p. 215.

is superimposed "like a coping-stone,"[4] for its power of "seeing things as a whole."[5]

As ruthlessly selective in human material as in appropriate studies, Plato insists that the future guardians shall be steady in temperament, brave, diligent in study, high-minded, capable of rigorous self-discipline, and physically tough.

Dewey speaks last on the theme of education as the basis of social order, differing from Plato in a number of crucial respects. First, Dewey's notion of educational preparation encompasses every individual, not a selected few. Second, his ends-in-view all lie within the educational process, not outside it in the perfect state. The individual is not to be prepared for a final end—whether it be that of a "complete philosopher" or of a stable society—but is to use past and present experience in an intelligent adjustment to life situations, continuously striving to improve the quality of his experience. Third, Dewey speaks for freedom founded on intelligent individual observations and judgments, as opposed to the static, strait-jacket-like ordering of the Platonic system. Fourth, as the surest way to understand social problems, Dewey advocates an introduction to problem-solving scientific method, not in the abstract mathematical and logical manner of Plato's design for guardians, but "through acquaintance with everyday social applications." Fifth, Dewey counters Plato's narrow prescription of subject matter with a concept of a progressive organization of subject matter arising from intelligent, cumulative observations of experience.

[4] Ibid., 230.
[5] Ibid., p. 233.

The Relation of the Individual to the State

Plato: On the Individual and the State[1]

(The dialogue is between Socrates and Glaucon. Socrates speaks first.)

'Can we mention any greater evil to a city than that which rends it asunder and makes it not one city but many? or any greater good than that which binds it together and makes it one?'

'We cannot.'

'Then does not communion in pleasure and pain bind the city together, when, as far as may be, all the citizens rejoice and grieve alike over the same births and the same deaths?'

'Certainly.'

'On the other hand, is not individuality in these feelings a dissolving force, when one part of the citizens are smitten with grief and the other transported with joy over the same experiences of the city or its inhabitants?'

'Surely.'

'And does not this state of things result when such words as "mine" and "not mine," "another's" and "not another's," are not pronounced in the city in concert?'

'Yes, indeed.'

'Then that city is best governed, whichever it may be, in which the largest number of men agree in applying these words, "mine" or "not mine," to the same thing?'

'Very much so.'

'And is it not this that is nearest the condition of a single individual? For consider, when any of us hurts his finger, the whole fellowship of body and soul which is bound into a single organization, namely, that of the ruling power within it, feels the hurt, and is all in pain at once, whole and hurt part together. And so we say that the man has a pain in his finger. And in regard to any part of the human body whatever, may not the same account be given of the pain felt when a part is hurt, and of the pleasure felt when it is at ease?'

'Yes,' he said. 'And to return to your question, the life of the best governed city comes very near to this condition.'

'Then I fancy that when an individual citizen has any experience,

[1] From Plato, *The Republic,* translated by Dr. A. D. Lindsay. Everyman's Library Edition. London: J. M. Dent & Sons, 1935, Book V, pp. 152-155, with omissions. Reprinted by permission of E. P. Dutton & Co., Inc.

whether good or bad, such a city will most certainly declare that experience its own, and the whole city will share his joy or his sorrow.'

'That must certainly be the case if the city has good laws," he said.

'It will now be time for us,' I said, 'to return to our own city and examine whether in it we shall find the conclusions of our argument most strikingly realized, or whether in this point some other city surpasses it.'

'Yes, we must do so,' he said.

'Well, then, in this city, as in the rest, there are rulers and people, are there not?'

'Yes.'

'And do not these all call each other citizens?'

'Surely.'

'But in other cities, what do the people call the rulers besides citizens?'

'In many cities they call them masters, but in democratic cities simply rulers.'

'What of the people in our city? What do they call the rulers besides citizens?'

'Saviours and helpers,' he said.

'And what do these call the people?'

'Wage payers and supporters.'

'But what do the rulers in other cities call the people?'

'Slaves,' he said.

'And what do the rulers call each other?'

'Fellow-rulers,' he said.

'And in our city?'

'Fellow-guardians.'

*   *   *   *

'Then in this city above all others, when any one meets with good fortune or with bad they will join in uttering the words which I have just spoken, saying "It is well with mine" or "It is ill with mine.' "

'Very true,' he said.

'Did we not say that upon this belief and its expression followed a community in pleasures and pains?'

'We did, and we were right.'

'Then will not our citizens most truly have community in the same thing, that to which they will apply the name "mine," and having such community, will they not most truly have community of pleasure and pain?'

'Certainly.'

'And besides the general arrangements of the state, is not the guardians' community of wives and children a cause of this?'

'Most certainly it is,' he said.

'But you remember that when we likened a well established city to the relation of a body and its members in its feelings of pleasure and pain, we agreed that this was the greatest good that could come to it.'

'And we were right,' he said.

'Then we have proved the auxiliaries' community of wives and children to be a cause of the greatest good that a city can have?'

'Certainly we have,' he said.

'Then in this we are also consistent with our former remarks. For we said, did we not, that if they were to be guardians in reality they must not have houses or land or any other possession of their own, but must receive what they need for sustenance from the other citizens as wages for their guardianship, and lay it out in common?'

'We were right,' he said.

'Then am I correct in saying that these regulations, together with our former statements, will do still more to make them true guardians, and prevent the disruption of the city which would result if each man gave the name of "mine" not to the same but to different things; if all took what they could get for themselves, and dragged it off to their different private houses; if each called a different wife and different children his own, and thus implanted in the city the individual pleasures and griefs of individuals: rather they will have one single belief concerning what is their own and be all concerned in the same purpose, and so will all be, as far as is possible, simultaneously affected by pleasure and pain?'

'That is perfectly true,' he said.

'Further, will not lawsuits and prosecutions almost have disappeared if their own persons are their only private property and everything else is common? Will they not, therefore, be free from all those quarrels that arise among men from the possession of money, or children, or kinsmen?'

'It is quite inevitable that they should,' he said.

Sir Percy Nunn: The Aim of Education[1]

It[2] is a trite remark that man is a social animal, and that the 'herd instinct' that makes him such is the source of all civilization and of all

[1] From Sir Percy Nunn, *Education: Its Data and First Principles*. London: Edward Arnold (Publishers) Ltd., 3rd edition, 1945, pp. 11-17, with omissions. Reprinted by permission of Edward Arnold (Publishers) Ltd.

[2] The following paragraph is quoted from a chapter contributed by the author to *Educating for Democracy*, edited by J. L. Cohen and R. M. W. Travers (Macmillan, 1939).

human worth. There is little need to restate the arguments that lead to this far-reaching conclusion; it is sufficiently plain that a man becomes what he becomes mainly as the result of his reactions to his social environment—the influence upon him of intercourse with parents and brethren, of schoolfellows and schoolmasters, companions and rivals, friends and enemies, employers and employees. It is, moreover, easy to recognize the deep influence which the 'social heritage'—the whole body of traditions and institutions of a people—has upon the growth and structure of the individual mind. To deny or to seek to minimize these patent facts would be to exhibit a strange blindness to reality; yet when the inferences that too many thinkers have drawn from them are considered, one sees that one's admissions must be carefully safeguarded. It does not follow that a community has a 'universal mind,' except in a metaphorical or Pickwickian sense of the term; the only minds that actually exist are the minds of the individual citizens. It does not follow that the whole function of the individual is to serve the interests or add to the glory of the great Leviathan, the alleged communal Person. Philosophers or politicians who argue in these senses allow themselves to be misled by a dangerous and pernicious inversion of values: they value the mould above the thing moulded; they speak as if the gold existed for the sake of the guinea-stamp and not the stamp for the sake of making the gold a guinea. The instinct behind the democratic idea rejects this attitude. It recognizes (of course) that national traditions and institutions have a permanence that makes the individual life seem a trivial thing. It recognizes that those are often noble and august and that this is only too often, as Hobbes's phrase runs, poor, nasty, and brutish as well as short. Yet it feels that national traditions and institutions are important only because they help to fashion desirable patterns of individual life, and refuses to lose its sense of reality in face of their impressive grandeur. The instinct that points this way is, one must believe, a sound one; and if it is sound there is no doubt about the educational canon that follows from it. We must hold that a scheme of education is ultimately to be valued by its success in fostering the highest degrees of individual excellence of which those submitted to it are capable.

Such a doctrine we seek to set out in these pages and to make the basis of a stable educational policy. We shall stand throughout on the position that nothing good enters into the human world except in and through the free activities of individual men and women, and that educational practice must be shaped to accord with that truth. This view does not deny or minimize the responsibilities of a man to his fellows; for the individual life can develop only in terms of its own nature, and that is social as truly as it is 'self-regarding.' Nor does it deny the value of tradition and discipline or exclude the influences of religion. But it does deny the reality of any super-personal entity of which the single life, taken by itself, is but an insignificant element. It reaffirms the infinite value of the individual person; it reasserts his ultimate responsibility for his own destiny; and it accepts all the practical corollaries that assertion implies.

Returning to an earlier remark, we may state the position in another way. While every man tends to draw his ideal of life largely from the inspiration of others, yet it may be maintained that, in a perfectly good sense of the words, each must have his own unique ideal. It is the sense in which every work of art—for instance, every poem—has its own ideal. A poet who recognizes that his creative impulse has failed would never point to another poem and say, 'That is what I intended to do.' His ideal was concrete, and to be embodied, if at all, in *his* poem and in no other. It marks the perfect achievement from which *his* work has fallen short; not a goal that another has or might have reached. It follows that there can be no universal aim of education if that aim is to include the assertion of any particular ideal of life; for there are as many ideals as there are persons. Educational efforts must, it would seem, be limited to securing for every one of the conditions under which individuality is most completely developed—that is to enabling him to make his original contribution to the variegated whole of human life as full and as truly characteristic as his nature permits; the form of the contribution being left to the individual as something which each must, in living and by living, forge out for himself.

*   *   *   *

Social obligations can be discharged in an infinite number of ways, and none can foresee or set bounds to what the human spirit may do in this as in the other fields of its activity. A daring and powerful soul may raise the whole moral quality of the social structure by asserting an individuality that may at first seem hostile to its very existence. And the unheroic soul, too, will best serve society by becoming more fully and truly himself. In short, the claims of society upon its members are best satisfied, not when each is made as like his fellows as possible, but when, in Bosanquet's language, 'he values himself as the inheritor of the gifts and surroundings that are focused in him, and which it is his business to raise to their highest power.'

The reader may have noticed that we have so far not raised the question whether society (or, to be precise, the State) may not at times of crisis demand services that entail the supersession, even the final sacrifice, of individual development, and whether an affirmative answer would not greatly weaken the general force of our argument. We might reply that for numberless men during the last two terrible wars such a sacrifice was actually the heroic consummation of self-fulfilment; but that reply, although true, is (in the memorable words of Nurse Cavell) 'not enough.' We must take firmly the line that mankind is not condemned for ever to endure its present evils; if there is a will to escape from them, its nobler spirits will certainly find a way. But if it is lawful to dream of a world in which the good of all would be much more nearly the good of each than it is at present, it is lawful to do whatever may help to make the dream reality. What, then, could education do better than to strengthen men's sense of the worth of individuality, teaching them to esteem the individual life, not, indeed, as a private possession, but as the only means by which real value can enter the world? Here, it may be claimed, is the strongest bulwark of freedom and the firmest guarantee against the rule of violence.

Some who are satisfied that the intentions of our doctrine are good may yet doubt whether they are practicable. Does it not require, if not a separate school, at least a separate curriculum for every pupil? Here again we insist that we do not seek to change the unchangeable conditions of human existence, but merely to make the best use of them. Individuality develops only in a social atmosphere where it can feed on common interests and common activities. What G. K. Chesterton said about the artist is, in fact, true of every man: 'His attitude to his age is his individuality; men are never individual when alone.'[3] All we demand is that individuality shall have free scope, within the common life, to grow in its own way, and that it shall not be warped from its ideal bent by alien forces. Under such conditions some boys and girls will show themselves to be by nature secluded and cloistral spirits, and it is to the general interest that they should have license to be so. But the crowd and the hero have such potent influence that few are likely in their development to wander far from the established types. In short, individuality is by no means the same thing as eccentricity. Teachers are not called upon to manufacture it deliberately, but merely to let it grow unimpeded out of the materials of each child's nature, fashioned by whatever forces, strong or weak, that nature may include.

It is the common boast of Englishmen that throughout their history they have clung stubbornly to individual liberty and have refused to exchange it for any more specious but delusive good. The worst charge

[3] *The Victorian Age in Literature* (Home Univ. Libr.), p. 10.

that can be brought against them is that in refusing equal liberty to others they have sometimes sinned against the light that is in them. Upon what basis does that historic claim to liberty rest if not upon the truth, seen darkly by some, by others clearly envisaged, that freedom for each to conduct life's adventure in his own way and to make the best he can of it is the one universal ideal sanctioned by nature and approved by reason?

Individual Differences Among Citizens

Plato: On Individual Differences among Citizens[1]

(Here the dialogue is between Socrates, who speaks first, and Adeimantus.)

'The origin of a city,' I said, 'is, in my opinion, due to the fact that no one of us is sufficient for himself, but each is in need of many things. Or do you think there is any other cause for the founding of cities?'

'No,' he said, 'none.'

'Then men, being in want of many things, gather into one settlement many partners and helpers; one taking to himself one man, and another another, to satisfy their diverse needs, and to this common settlement we give the name of city. Is not that so?'

'Certainly.'

'And when they exchange with one another, giving or receiving as the case may be, does not each man think that such exchange is to his own good?'

'Certainly.'

'Come, then,' I said. 'Let us in our argument construct the city from the beginning. Apparently it will be the outcome of our need?'

'Surely.'

'But the first and greatest of our needs is the provision of food to support existence and life?"

'Yes, assuredly.'

'The second the provision of a dwelling-place, and the third of clothing, and so on?'

'That is so.'

'Come, then,' I said, 'how will our city be able to supply a sufficiency of all those things? Will it not be by having one man a farmer, another a builder, and a third a weaver? Shall we add a shoemaker, and perhaps another provider of bodily needs?'

'Certainly.'

'Then the city of bare necessity will consist of four or five men?'

'Apparently.'

'Well, then, should each of these men place his own work at the

---

[1] From Plato, *The Republic*, translated by Dr. A. D. Lindsay, Everyman's Library Edition. London: J. M. Dent & Sons, 1935, Book II, pp. 47-49; Book IV p. 121; Book IX, pp. 280-283, with omissions. Reprinted by permission of E. P. Dutton & Co., Inc.

disposal of all in common? For example, should our one farmer provide corn for four and spend fourfold time and labour on the provision of corn, and then share it with the rest; or should he pay no attention to the others, and provide only a fourth part of the corn for himself in a fourth of the time, and spend the other three-fourths of his time in providing a house, clothes, and shoes? Should he not have the trouble of sharing with the others, but rather provide with his own hands what he wants for himself?'

Adeimantus answered: 'The first alternative, Socrates, is perhaps the easier.'

'Well, it is certainly not strange that it is. For as you were speaking, I myself was thinking that, in the first place, no two of us are by nature altogether alike. Our capacities differ. Some are fit for one work, some for another. Do you agree?'

'I do.'

'Well, then, would better work be done on the principle of one man many trades, or of one man one trade?'

'One man one trade is better,' he said.

'Yes, for I fancy that it is also evident that, in work, opportunities which we pass by are lost.'

'That is evident.'

'I fancy that things to be done will not wait the good time of the doer. Rather the doer must wait on the opportunity for action, and not leave the doing of it for his idle moments.'

'He must.'

'And so more tasks of each kind are accomplished, and the work is better and is done more easily when each man works at the one craft for which nature fits him, that being free from all other occupations he may wait on its opportunities.'

'That is certainly the case.'

'Then, Adeimantus, we need more citizens than four to provide the above-mentioned necessities. For the farmer, naturally, will not make his own plough if it is to be a good one, nor his mattock, nor any of the other farming tools. No more will the builder, who also needs many tools. And the same will hold of the weaver and the shoemaker, will it not?'

'True.'

'Then carpenters and smiths and many other artisans of that kind will become members of our little city, and make it populous?'

'Certainly.'

*   *   *   *

(Socrates is now speaking with Glaucon.)

'Consider, now, whether you agree with me. Do you think it will do any notable harm to the city if a builder attempts a shoemaker's work, or a shoemaker a builder's, or if they take one another's tools or pay, or even if the same man try to do both, and there is a general interchange in such professions?'

'No,' he said.

'But I fancy when he that is by nature a craftsman or a money-maker of some kind is so elated by his wealth, or his numerous sup-porters, or his bodily strength, or some such qualities, that he essays to enter the warrior class; or when one of the warriors aspires to the coun-selling and guardian class when he is unworthy of it, and these take one another's tools and privileges, or when the same man tries to combine all these offices, then, I fancy, you think with me that such change and meddling among those classes is death to the city?'

'Most certainly.'

'Our classes are three, and meddling and interchange among them is the greatest of injuries to the city, and might justly be described as the extreme of evil-doing.'

'It is exactly as you say.'

'Then will you not admit that the worst kind of evil-doing to one's own city is injustice?'

'Surely.'

'This then is injustice; and conversely the opposite of this—when each class, money-makers, auxiliaries, and guardians, attends to what belongs to it, each doing its own work in the city—will be justice, and will make the city just.'

*   *   *   *

'Since the soul of each individual,' I said, 'is, like the city, divided into three forms, it will admit, I think, of yet another demonstration.'

'What is it?'

'It is this. Belonging to these three forms there appear to me to be three pleasures, one special pleasure attaching to each particular form, and so with desires and principles of rule.'

'What do you mean?' he said.

'There is, first, that by which a man learns,' I said; 'secondly, that by which he is angry. The third contains such varied forms within it that we could find no one special name for it, but named it after the greatest and strongest thing in it. For we called it the desiring form because of the intensity of the desires concerned with food and drink and sex and so on; and we also called it money-loving, because such desires are usually satisfied with the help of money.'

'And we were right,' he said.

'And if we were further to say that its pleasure and love is in gain, would not that be our best way of getting a satisfactory general expression to use in our argument, so that we should know what we were talking about when we referred to this part of the soul; and if we named it the money-loving or the gain-loving form, should we not be right?'

'I certainly think so,' he said.

'Further, did we not say that the spirited element is ever wholly bent on mastery and victory and fame?'

'We did.'

'Then should we be right in calling it the victory-loving and the honour-loving form?'

'Quite right.'

'And, lastly, as to the part with which we learn, it is obvious to every one that it is for ever straining to know where the truth lies, and cares for money and reputation less than the others.'

'Yes, much less.'

'Will it be right if we call it learning-loving and philosophic?'

'Surely.'

'And men's hearts,' I said, 'are ruled, are they not, some by this last element, others by one of the other two, as the case may be?'

'That is so,' he said.

'Then it is for these reasons that we say that of men also there are three primary classes—the lovers of wisdom, the lovers of victory, and the lovers of gain?'

'Exactly so.'

'Then there are also three kinds of pleasures, one for each of the three?'

'Yes.'

'Now do you know,' I said, 'that if you were to ask three such men, each in turn, which of these lives is the most pleasant, each would extol his own life most highly? The money-maker will say, will he not, that, compared with the pleasures of gain, the pleasures of honour or of learning are worthless except in so far as they bring in money?'

'True,' he said.

'And is not the lover of honour the same?' I said. 'Does he not consider that the pleasures of money-making are rather vulgar, and those of learning, on the other hand, except in so far as learning brings honour, mere smoke and nonsense?'

'That is so,' he said.

'Then how shall we imagine that the philosopher regards the other pleasures in comparison with the pleasure of knowing where the truth lies and of being always in a state akin to knowledge when he is learning? For him there can be no comparison, can there? He will call the others in good truth compulsory pleasures. He has no need for them, but they are forced upon him.'

'Should we not make quite certain of that?' he said.

'Well,' I said, 'when the discussion concerns the pleasures, and in fact the whole life, of each type of man, and the question at issue is not their relative nobility or disgracefulness, their goodness or badness, but simply and solely which is most pleasant and least painful, how can we know which of the three speaks most truly?'

'I can't say,' he said.

'Well, look at the matter in this way. What is wanted for a judgment that is to turn out to be right? Is it not experience and insight and reason? Can you have any better test than these?'

'Of course not,' he said.

'Now, consider. There are those three men. Which of them has had most experience of all these pleasures? Do you think that the gain-lover learns the nature of truth and acquires more experience of the pleasure of knowledge than the philosopher has of the pleasure of gain?'

'The cases are very different,' he said. 'For the latter must of necessity start in childhood by testing both the other kinds; whereas there is no compulsion on the gain-lover to learn the nature of reality and taste the sweetness of this pleasure or to have any experience of it. Nay, if he had the best will in the world, he would find it no easy matter.'

'Then the philosopher,' I said, 'far excels the gain-lover in his experience of both pleasures?'

'Yes.'

'And the lover of honour also? Or has he less experience of the pleasures of honour than the other has of the pleasure derived from wisdom?'

'No,' he said, 'honour comes to them all if they accomplish their several aims. For the rich man is honoured by many. So is the brave and the wise man. So that all have experience of the pleasure which comes from being honoured and know its nature; but it is impossible for any one but the philosopher to taste the pleasure contained in the vision of being.'

'Then so far as experience is concerned,' I said, 'he will judge best of the three men?'

'Far the best.'

'And his experience alone will involve insight?'

'Certainly.'

'And, lastly, as to the necessary instrument of judgment, it is not the instrument of the gain-lover or of the honour-lover, but of the philosopher?'

'What is that instrument?'

'Surely we said that judgment must be made by means of reasoning?'

'Yes.'

'But reasoning is this man's especial instrument?'

'Surely.'

'Now, if what is being judged were best judged by means of wealth and profit, the praise and blame of the gain-lover would necessarily be the truest?'

'Necessarily.'

'Or if by means of honour and victory and courage, the praise of the honour- and victory-lover would be truest?'

'Obviously.'

'But since they are best judged by means of experience and insight and reason——?'

'It is inevitable,' he said, 'that the praise of the philosopher and lover of reason should be truest.'

'Then of these three pleasures, will not that be the pleasantest which belongs to the part of the soul wherewith we learn, and pleasantest also the life of him amongst us in whom this part rules?'

'How else?' he said. 'The wise man's praise is decisive, and he praises his own life.'

'What life and what pleasure does the judge declare to come second?'

'Obviously the pleasure of the warrior and the honour-lover, for that is nearer him than the pleasure of the money-maker.'

'Then the gain-lover's apparently comes last?'

'Of course,' he said.

John Dewey: The Platonic Educational Philosophy[1]

No one could better express than did [Plato] the fact that a society is stably organized when each individual is doing that for which he has aptitude by nature in such a way as to be useful to others (or to contribute to the whole to which he belongs); and that it is the business

[1] John Dewey, *Democracy and Education.* New York: The Free Press of Glencoe, paperback edition, 1966, pp. 81-83, 86-88, 89-91, with omissions. Reprinted by permission of The Macmillan Company, copyright 1916 The Macmillan Company; renewed 1944 by John Dewey.

of education to discover these aptitudes and progressively to train them for social use. Much which has been said so far is borrowed from what Plato first consciously taught the world. But conditions which he could not intellectually control led him to restrict these ideas in their application. He never got any conception of the indefinite plurality of activities which may characterize an individual and a social group, and consequently limited his view to a limited number of *classes* of capacities and of social arrangements.

Plato's starting point is that the organization of society depends ultimately upon knowledge of the end of existence. If we do not know its end, we shall be at the mercy of accident and caprice. Unless we know the end, the good, we shall have no criterion for rationally deciding what the possibilities are which should be promoted, nor how social arrangements are to be ordered. We shall have no conception of the proper limits and distribution of activities—what he called justice —as a trait of both individual and social organization. But how is the knowledge of the final and permanent good to be achieved? In dealing with this question we come upon the seemingly insuperable obstacle that such knowledge is not possible save in a just and harmonious social order. Everywhere else the mind is distracted and misled by false valuations and false perspectives. A disorganized and factional society sets up a number of different models and standards. Under such conditions it is impossible for the individual to attain consistency of mind. Only a complete whole is fully self-consistent. A society which rests upon the supremacy of some factor over another irrespective of its rational or proportionate claims, inevitably leads thought astray. It puts a premium on certain things and slurs over others, and creates a mind whose seeming unity is forced and distorted. Education proceeds ultimately from the patterns furnished by institutions, customs, and laws. Only in a just state will these be such as to give the right education; and only those who have rightly trained minds will be able to recognize the end, and ordering principle of things. We seem to be caught in a hopeless circle. However, Plato suggested a way out. A few men, philosophers or lovers of wisdom—or truth—may by study learn at least in outline the proper patterns of true existence. If a powerful ruler should form a state after these patterns, then its regulations could be preserved. An education could be given which would sift individuals, discovering what they were good for, and supplying a method of assigning each to the work in life for which his nature fits him. Each doing his own part, and never transgressing, the order and unity of the whole would be maintained.

It would be impossible to find in any scheme of philosophic

thought a more adequate recognition on one hand of the educational significance of social arrangements and, on the other, of the dependence of those arrangements upon the means used to educate the young. It would be impossible to find a deeper sense of the function of education in discovering and developing personal capacities, and training them so that they would connect with the activities of others. Yet the society in which the theory was propounded was so undemocratic that Plato could not work out a solution for the problem whose terms he clearly saw.

While he affirmed with emphasis that the place of the individual in society should not be determined by birth or wealth or any conventional status, but by his own nature as discovered in the process of education, he had no perception of the uniqueness of individuals. For him they fall by nature into classes, and into a very small number of classes at that. Consequently the testing and sifting function of education only shows to which one of three classes an individual belongs. There being no recognition that each individual constitutes his own class, there could be no recognition of the infinite diversity of active tendencies and combinations of tendencies of which an individual is capable. There were only three types of faculties or powers in the individual's constitution. Hence education would soon reach a static limit in each class, for only diversity makes change and progress.

In some individuals, appetites naturally dominate; they are assigned to the laboring and trading class, which expresses and supplies human wants. Others reveal, upon education, that over and above appetites, they have a generous, outgoing, assertively courageous disposition. They become the citizen-subjects of the state; its defenders in war; its internal guardians in peace. But their limit is fixed by their lack of reason, which is a capacity to grasp the universal. Those who possess this are capable of the highest kind of education, and become in time the legislators of the state—for laws are the universals which control the particulars of experience. Thus it is not true that in intent, Plato subordinated the individual to the social whole. But it is true that lacking the perception of the uniqueness of every individual, his incommensurability with others, and consequently not recognizing that a society might change and yet be stable, his doctrine of limited powers and classes came in net effect to the idea of the subordination of individuality.

We cannot better Plato's conviction that an individual is happy and society well organized when each individual engages in those activities for which he has a natural equipment, nor his conviction that it is the primary office of education to discover this equipment to its possessor and train him for its effective use. But progress in knowledge has made us aware of the superficiality of Plato's lumping of individuals and their original powers into a few sharply marked-off classes; it has taught us that original capacities are indefinitely numerous and variable. It is but the other side of this fact to say that in the degree in which society has become democratic, social organization means utilization of the specific and variable qualities of individuals, not stratification by classes. Although his educational philosophy was revolutionary, it was none the less in bondage to static ideals. He thought that change or alteration was evidence of lawless flux; that true reality was unchangeable. Hence while he would radically change the existing state of society, his aim was to construct a state in which change would subsequently have no place. The final end of life is fixed; given a state framed with this end in view, not even minor details are to be altered. Though they might not be inherently important, yet if permitted they would inure the minds of men to the idea of change, and hence be dissolving and anarchic. The breakdown of his philosophy is made apparent in the fact that he could not trust to gradual improvements in education to bring about a better society which should then improve education, and so on indefinitely. Correct education could not come into existence until an ideal state existed, and after that education would be devoted simply to its conservation. For the existence of this state he was obliged to trust to some happy accident by which philosophic wisdom should happen to coincide with possession of ruling power in the state.

*   *   *   *

(Dewey now proposes his own democratic conception in education.)

Society is one word, but many things. Men associate together in all kinds of ways and for all kinds of purposes. One man is concerned in a multitude of diverse groups, in which his associates may be quite different. It often seems as if they had nothing in common except that they are modes of associated life. Within every larger social organization there are numerous minor groups: not only political subdivisions, but industrial, scientific, religious, associations. There are political parties with differing aims, social sets, cliques, gangs, corporations, partnerships, groups bound closely together by ties of blood, and so on in endless variety. In many modern states and in some ancient, there is great diversity of populations, of varying languages, religions, moral codes, and traditions. From this standpoint, many a minor political unit, one of our large cities, for example, is a congeries of loosely associated societies, rather than an inclusive and permeating community of action and thought.

The terms society, community, are thus ambiguous. They have both a eulogistic or normative sense, and a descriptive sense; a meaning *de jure* and a meaning *de facto*. In social philosophy, the former connotation is almost always uppermost. Society is conceived as one by its very nature. The qualities which accompany this unity, praiseworthy community of purpose and welfare, loyalty to public ends, mutuality of sympathy, are emphasized. But when we look at the facts which the term *denotes* instead of confining our attention to its intrinsic *connotation,* we find not unity, but a plurality of societies, good and bad. Men banded together in a criminal conspiracy, business aggregations that prey upon the public while serving it, political machines held together by the interest of plunder, are included. If it is said that such organizations are not societies because they do not meet the ideal requirements of the notion of society, the answer, in part, is that the conception of society is then made so "ideal" as to be of no use, having no reference to facts; and in part, that each of these organizations, no matter how opposed to the interests of other groups, has something of the praiseworthy qualities of "Society" which hold it together. There is honor among thieves, and a band of robbers has a common interest as respects its members. Gangs are marked by fraternal feeling, and narrow cliques by intense loyalty to their own codes. Family life may be marked by exclusiveness, suspicion, and jealousy as to those without, and yet be a model of amity and mutual aid within. Any education given by a group tends to socialize its members, but the quality and value of the socialization depends upon the habits and aims of the group.

Hence, once more, the need of a measure for the worth of any given mode of social life. In seeking this measure, we have to avoid two extremes. We cannot set up, out of our heads, something we regard as an ideal society. We must base our conception upon societies which actually exist, in order to have any assurance that our ideal is a practicable one. But, as we have just seen, the ideal cannot simply repeat the traits which are actually found. The problem is to extract the desirable traits of forms of community life which actually exist, and employ them to criticize undesirable features and suggest improvement. Now in any social group whatever, even in a gang of thieves, we find some interest held in common, and we find a certain amount of interaction and coöperative intercourse with other groups. From these two traits we derive our standard. How numerous and varied are the interests which are consciously shared? How full and free is the interplay with other forms of association? If we apply these considerations to, say, a criminal band, we find that the ties which consciously hold the members together are few in number, reducible almost to a common interest in plunder; and that they are of such a nature as to isolate the group from other groups with respect to give and take of the values of life. Hence, the education such a society gives is partial and distorted. If we take, on the other hand, the kind of family life which illustrates the standard, we find that there are material, intellectual, æsthetic interests in which all participate and that the progress of one member has worth for the experience of other members—it is readily communicable—and that the family is not an isolated whole, but enters intimately into relationships with business groups, with schools, with all the agencies of culture, as well as with other similar groups, and that it plays a due part in the political organization and in return receives support from it. In short, there are many interests consciously communicated and shared; and there are varied and free points of contact with other modes of association.

*   *   *   *

The Democratic Ideal.   The two elements in our criterion both point to democracy. The first signifies not only more numerous and more varied points of shared common interest, but greater reliance upon the recognition of mutual interests as a factor in social control. The second means not only freer interaction between social groups (once isolated so far as intention could keep up a separation) but change in social habit—its continuous readjustment through meeting the new situations produced by varied intercourse. And these two traits are precisely what characterize the democratically constituted society.

Upon the educational side, we note first that the realization of a form of social life in which interests are mutually interpenetrating, and where progress, or readjustment, is an important consideration, makes a democratic community more interested than other communities have cause to be in deliberate and systematic education. The devotion of democracy to education is a familiar fact. The superficial explanation is that a government resting upon popular suffrage cannot be successful unless those who elect and who obey their governors are educated. Since a democratic society repudiates the principle of external authority, it must find a substitute in voluntary disposition and interest; these can be created only by education. But there is a deeper explanation. A democracy is more than a form of government; it is primarily a mode of associated living, of conjoint communicated experience. The extension in space of the number of individuals who participate in an interest so that each has to refer his own action to that of others, and to consider the action of others to give point and direction to his own, is equivalent to the breaking down of those barriers of class, race, and national territory which kept men from perceiving the full import of their activity. These more numerous and more varied points of contact denote a greater diversity of stimuli to which an individual has to respond; they consequently put a premium on variation in his action. They secure a liberation of powers which remain suppressed as long as the incitations to action are partial, as they must be in a group which in its exclusiveness shuts out many interests.

The widening of the area of shared concerns, and the liberation of a greater diversity of personal capacities which characterize a democracy, are not of course the product of deliberation and conscious effort. On the contrary, they were caused by the development of modes of manufacture and commerce, travel, migration, and intercommunication which flowed from the command of science over natural energy. But after greater individualization on one hand, and a broader community of interest on the other have come into existence, it is a matter of deliberate effort to sustain and extend them. Obviously a society to which stratification into separate classes would be fatal, must see to it that intellectual opportunities are accessible to all on equable and easy terms. A society marked off into classes need be specially attentive only to the education of its ruling elements. A society which is mobile, which is full of channels for the distribution of a change occurring anywhere, must see to it that its members are educated to personal initiative and adaptability. Otherwise, they will be overwhelmed by the changes in which they are caught and whose significance or connections they do not perceive. The result will be a confusion in which a few will appropriate to themselves the results of the blind and externally directed activities of others.

Education as the Basis of the Social Order

Plato: Education as the Basis of the Social Order[1]

(Socrates discusses with Glaucon the subjects most befitting the preparation of philosopher-rulers.)

'But calculation and arithmetic are throughout concerned with number?'

'Certainly.'

'Then they are seen to lead towards truth?'

'Yes, in a pre-eminent degree.'

'Then here apparently we have one of the studies which we are seeking. For this study is essential to a warrior for his drill, and to a philosopher, because he must rise above becoming and lay hold on being if he is ever to become a reasonable arithmetician.'

'That is so,' he said.

'But our guardian is both warrior and philosopher?'

'Surely.'

'Then it will be fitting, Glaucon, to prescribe this study by law, and to persuade those who are to share in the highest affairs of the city to take to calculation, and embrace it in no amateur spirit. They must go on until they arrive by the help of sheer intelligence at a vision of the nature of numbers, practising it not like merchants and pedlars for the sake of buying and selling, but for the purposes of war, and of an easier conversion of the soul itself from becoming to truth and being.'

'Most excellent words,' he said.

'Further it strikes me,' I said, 'now that we have mentioned the study of calculation, how elegant it is and in what manifold ways it helps our desires if it is pursued not for commercial ends but for the sake of knowledge.'

'In what way?' he said.

'In this way which we have just been mentioning. It powerfully draws the soul above, and forces it to reason concerning the numbers themselves, not allowing any discussion which presents to the soul numbers with bodies that can be seen or touched. You know how it is with skilled mathematicians? If any one in an argument attempts to dissect the one, they laugh at him, and will not allow it. If you cut it up, they

[1] From Plato, *The Republic,* translated by Dr. A. D. Lindsay. Everyman's Library Edition. London: J. M. Dent & Sons, 1935, Book VII, pp. 212-214, 219-221, 224-231, 236. Reprinted by permission of E. P. Dutton & Co., Inc.

multiply it, taking good care that the one shall never appear not as one but as many parts.'

'That is perfectly true.'

'Then what, Glaucon, if you were to say to them, "My wonderful friend, what sort of numbers are you discussing in which the one answers your claims, in which each 'one' is equal to every other 'one' without the smallest difference and contains within itself no parts?" How do you think they would reply?'

'I fancy by saying that they are talking about those numbers which can be apprehended by the understanding alone, but in no other way.'

'Do you see, then, my friend,' I said, 'that this study may fairly be thought necessary for us, since we find that it necessitates that the soul shall apply intelligence itself to truth itself?'

'Yes, indeed,' he said; "it does that in a very marked degree.'

'Further, have you ever noticed that those who have a natural capacity for calculation are, generally speaking, naturally quick at all kinds of study; while men of slow intellect, if they are trained and exercised in arithmetic, if they get nothing else from it, at least all improve and become sharper than they were before?'

'That is so,' he said.

'And I fancy you will not easily find many studies which are more trouble to learn and practice than this one?'

'No.'

'Then for all these reasons we must not neglect the study, but those who have the best natures must be trained in it?'

'I agree,' he said.

'Then let that be one point settled,' I said. 'Secondly, let us examine whether the study which borders on arithmetic suits us.'

'What is that?' he said. 'Do you mean geometry?'

'Just that,' I said.

'Obviously,' he said, 'so much of it as applies to warlike operations is suitable. In pitching camp, occupying positions, closing up or deploying an army, and generally in executing other manœuvres on the field of battle or on the march, it will make a difference whether a man is a geometrician or not.'

'Yes,' I said, 'but for such purposes quite a little geometry and calculation is sufficient. For the greater and the more advanced portion we must consider whether it tends to the other result, to making it easier to perceive the Form of the good. All things have this tendency, we say, if they compel the soul to turn towards that region which contains that most blissful sphere of being which it is most necessary for the soul to see.'

'You are right,' he said.

'Then if it compels us to behold being, it is suitable; if to behold becoming, it is unsuitable?'

'That is our statement.'

'But none who have even a slight acquaintance with geometry,' I said, 'will deny that the nature of this science is in exact contradiction to the arguments used in it by its professors.'

'In what way?' he asked.

'Well, they talk in most ridiculous and beggarly fashion; for they speak like men of business, and as though all their demonstrations had a practical aim, with their talk of squaring and applying and adding, and so on. But surely the whole study is carried on for the sake of knowledge.'

'Most certainly,' he said.

'Then must we not admit this further point?'

'What?'

'That it is for the knowledge of that which always is, not of that which at some particular place and time is becoming and perishing.'

'That may well be agreed,' he said. 'For geometrical knowledge is of that which always is.'

'Then, my fine fellow, it will draw the souls towards truth and complete the philosophic understanding, making us raise upwards what now we wrongly direct downwards?'

* * * *

... What then did you mean by saying that astronomy ought to be studied on a system very different from the present one, if its students were to learn anything of value for our purposes?'

'This,' I said. 'These ornaments of the heavens, since they adorn a visible sky, should be thought to be the most beautiful and to have the most perfect nature amongst visible things, but to fall far short of those true adornments, those movements wherewith pure velocity and pure retardation, in true number and in all true figures, are moved in relation to each other, and wherewith they also move that which is within them, which matters are to be apprehended by reason and understanding, but not by sight. Do you disagree?'

'Certainly not,' he said.

'Then,' I said, 'we must use the adornments of heaven as models in our study of those true ornaments, as though we had come across diagrams drawn and elaborated with surpassing skill by Daedalus or some other artist or draughtsman. For surely any competent geometrician on seeing such diagrams would think that they were most beautifully executed, but would consider it ridiculous to examine them seriously with any hope of finding in them the truths of equality or duplicity or any other ratio.'

*   *   *   *

'Do we not know that all these studies are but the prelude of the real melody which is to be studied? You surely don't think that men who are clever in these sciences are dialecticians?'

'By heavens, no,' he said; 'at least a very few of those I have met.'

'But,' I said, 'do you think that men who are unable to give and receive reasons ever know anything of what we say they ought to know?'

'There again I answer no,' he said.

'Then, Glaucon,' I said, 'is this not at last the real melody played by dialectic? It is intelligible, and its copy is the power of sight which we described as at length endeavouring to look at the real animals, then at the real stars, and finally at the real sun. So too when any one tries by dialectic through the discourse of reason unaided by any of the senses to attain to what each reality is, and desists not until by sheer intelligence he apprehends the reality of good, then he stands at the real goal of the intelligible world, as the man in our simile stood at the goal of the visible.'

'Assuredly,' he said.

'Then do you not call this progress dialectic?'

'Yes.'

*   *   *   *

... We must give preference to the steadiest, the bravest, and, as far as possible, the best looking. But, further, we have not only to look out for men of noble and sturdy morals, they must also have natural gifts suitable for our scheme of education.'

'Then what do you determine these to be?'

'They must have keenness for their studies, my excellent friend,' I said, 'and find no difficulty in learning; for the soul plays the coward far more readily in severe study than in gymnastics. The exertion comes more home to it, being peculiar to itself, and not shared by the body.'

'True,' he said.

'The man of our search must also have a good memory, an unchangeable purpose, and an unflagging love of work. How else do you imagine that a man will consent to crown his bodily labours by all this study and practice?'

'No one but a man of exceptional natural abilities would do it,' he answered.

'Yes,' I said, 'the reason for men's mistaken view, and for the disgrace under which philosophy now suffers, is, as we said before, that men apply themselves to it without considering their unworthiness. But it should be the privilege only of the genuine sons of philosophy, not of bastards.'

'What do you mean?' he said.

'In the first place,' I said, 'he that is to study philosophy must not be lame in his love of work—zealous in the one half of it, and lazy in the other. And that is the description of a man who is fond of gymnastics and of hunting, and loves all bodily labours, but does not love study, is not fond of listening to others or of inquiring for himself, but hates any labour of that kind. And he whose love of work has taken the opposite direction is also halt.'

'That is most true,' he said.

'Similarly,' I said, 'in reference to truth, shall we not class as deformed a soul which, though it hates the lie told on purpose, and cannot endure it in itself, and is very angry when other people are deceitful, nevertheless is quite complacent to involuntary falsehood, and is not angry when it is found in a state of ignorance, but wallows in it like a bestial hog?'

'Most certainly,' he said.

'Then by reference to temperance,' I said, 'and courage, and high-mindedness, and all the elements of virtue we must most carefully distinguish between the true-born and the bastard. For if an individual or a city does not know how to observe carefully all these matters, they unwittingly employ cripples and bastards as friends or rulers in any of these services for which they have occasion.'

'Yes,' he said, 'that is certainly the case.'

'Then we must take all these precautions most carefully,' I said. 'Because if to this weighty study and severe discipline we bring men sound of limb and of sound mind, and train them therein, justice herself will find no fault with us, and we shall preserve the city and the constitution; but if we bring men of another stamp, the event will be in all respects the opposite, and we shall swamp philosophy in another flood of ridicule.'

* * * *

(Socrates explains to Glaucon the final emergence of the philosopher-rulers and their glimpses of the good.)

And when they are fifty, those who have come safely through, and have always triumphed throughout in word and deed, must at last be taken to the goal; they must be compelled to look upon that which gives light to all, and turn the gleam of their soul upon it and see the real good; then using that as the pattern for the rest of their life, they must take their turn in ordering city and individuals and their own lives; the most of their time they will spend in philosophy, but when their turn comes, they will endure the toil of directing politics and being rulers for the sake of their city, regarding such action not as anything noble but as a compulsion laid upon them; and so each generation, having trained up others like to themselves whom they can leave to be the city's guardians, will depart to the islands of the blest and dwell there. The city shall establish monuments and sacrifices to them, if the Pythian allows, honouring them as demigods, if not as happy and divine.'

*   *   *   *

'Then it will be our task as founders,' I said, 'to compel the best natures to proceed to that study which we declared a little while ago to be the highest, to perceive the good, and to make that ascent we spoke of,[1] and when they have done so, and looked long enough, then we must not allow them the liberty which they now enjoy.'

'What is that?'

'The liberty,' I said, 'of staying there, and refusing to descend again to the prisoners and to share with them in toils and honours, whether they be mean or exalted.'

'What!' he said; 'are we to do them an injustice, and force on them a worse life when a better is possible for them?'

'You have forgotten again, my friend,' I said, 'that it is not the law's concern that any one class in a state should live surpassingly well. Rather it contrives a good life for the whole state, harmonizing the citizens by persuasion and compulsion, and making them share with one another the advantage which each class can contribute to the community. It is the law which produces such men in the city; not in order to leave each man free to turn where he will, but that it may itself use them to bind the city together.'

'True,' he said, 'I had forgotten.'

---

[1] Socrates has earlier pictured men as prisoners in a cave, one of whom is able to make the ascent to the light of the world outside, symbolizing "the upward journey of the soul to the intelligible sphere" (p. 210) where *reality* can be glimpsed, in contrast with the mere *appearances* of things perceived in the everyday world (Editor's note).

'Consider further, Glaucon,' I said, 'that we shall not really do an injustice to the philosophers who arise in our city, but can speak justly when we proceed to compel them to watch over and care for the others. "It is quite reasonable," we shall say, "that the philosophers who arise in other cities should not share in their toils. For there they are spontaneous growths, and their city's constitution has only hampered them, and it seems fair that the self-sown plant which is debtor to no man for its culture should not be eager to pay the price of its culture to anybody. But you we have begotten for the city as well as for yourselves to be like leaders and kings in a hive. You have received a better and more thorough education than those other philosophers, and are more capable of participating in both public life and philosophy. You must, therefore, descend by turns to dwell with the rest of the city, and must be accustomed to see the dark objects; for when you are accustomed, you will be able to see a thousand times better than those who dwell there, and you will know what each of the images is, and of what it is an image, because you have seen the truth of what is beautiful and just and good. And so your and our city will become a waking reality, and not a dream like most existing cities, which are peopled by men fighting about shadows and quarrelling for office as though that were a notable good. Whereas the truth surely is this, that that city wherein those who are to rule are least anxious for office must have the best and most stable constitution, and where you have the contrary disposition in your rulers you will have the contrary result." '

'Certainly,' he said.

Then do you fancy that our nurselings when they hear this will disobey us, and will refuse to take their turn in sharing in the labours of the city, while for the most of their time they dwell with one another in the world of light?'

'Impossible,' he said. 'It is a just demand, and they are just. And assuredly each of them will take up office as a compulsory duty, reversing the attitude of those who now rule in cities.'

'Yes, that is so, my friend,' I said. 'If you can discover a life for those who are to rule, better than ruling, then for you a well-governed city is possible. For there alone the rulers will be those who are truly rich, not in money, but in the proper wealth of the happy man, a good and wise life. But this is impossible where men who are poor and hungry for goods of their own undertake public affairs, imagining that it is from these that their good is to be snatched; for then office becomes a thing to be fought for, and such a civil and intestine war destroys the combatants, and the whole state with them.'

John Dewey: The Meaning of Purpose[1]

What, then, is the true meaning of preparation in the educational scheme? In the first place, it means that a person, young or old, gets out of his present experience all that there is in it for him at the time in which he has it. When preparation is made the controlling end, then the potentialities of the present are sacrificed to a supposititious future. When this happens, the actual preparation for the future is missed or distorted. The ideal of using the present simply to get ready for the future contradicts itself. It omits, and even shuts out, the very conditions by which a person can be prepared for his future. We always live at the time we live and not at some other time, and only by extracting at each present time the full meaning of each present experience are we prepared for doing the same thing in the future. This is the only preparation which in the long run amounts to anything.

*   *   *   *

It is . . . a sound instinct which identifies freedom with power to frame purposes and to execute or carry into effect purposes so framed. Such freedom is in turn identical with self-control; for the formation of purposes and the organization of means to execute them are the work of intelligence. Plato once defined a slave as the person who executes the purposes of another, and . . . a person is also a slave who is enslaved to his own blind desires.

*   *   *   *

The formation of purposes is . . . a rather complex intellectual operation. It involves (1) observation of surrounding conditions; (2) knowledge of what has happened in similar situations in the past, a knowledge obtained partly by recollection and partly from the information, advice, and warning of those who have had a wider experience; and (3) judgment which puts together what is observed and what is recalled to see what they signify. A purpose differs from an original impulse and desire through its translation into a plan and method of action based upon foresight of the consequences of acting under given observed conditions in a certain way. "If wishes were horses, beggars would ride." Desire for something may be intense. It may be so strong

---

[1] From John Dewey, *Experience and Education.* New York: Collier Books, 1963 edition, pp. 49, 67-69, 80-81, with omissions. Copyright 1938 by Kappa Delta Pi; copyright renewed 1965 by Kappa Delta Pi and by Mrs. John Dewey. Reprinted by permission of Kappa Delta Pi and Mrs. John Dewey. (The views presented here complement Dewey's democratic conception in the selection above—Editor's note.)

as to override estimation of the consequences that will follow acting upon it. Such occurrences do not provide the model for education. The crucial educational problem is that of procuring the postponement of immediate action upon desire until observation and judgment have intervened. . . . Overemphasis upon activity as an end, instead of upon *intelligent* activity, leads to identification of freedom with immediate execution of impulses and desires. This identification is justified by a confusion of impulse with purpose; although, as has just been said, there is no purpose unless overt action is postponed until there is foresight of the consequences of carrying the impulse into execution—a foresight that is impossible without observation, information, and judgment. Mere foresight, even if it takes the form of accurate prediction, is not, of course, enough. The intellectual anticipation, the idea of consequences, must blend with desire and impulse to acquire moving force. It then gives direction to what otherwise is blind, while desire gives ideas, impetus, and momentum. An idea then becomes a plan in and for an activity to be carried out.

*   *   *   *

It is a sound educational principle that students should be introduced to scientific subject-matter and be initiated into its facts and laws through acquaintance with everyday social applications. Adherence to this method is not only the most direct avenue to understanding of science itself but as the pupils grow more mature it is also the surest road to the understanding of the economic and industrial problems of present society. For they are the products to a very large extent of the application of science in production and distribution of commodities and services, while the latter processes are the most important factor in determining the present relations of human beings and social groups to one another. It is absurd, then, to argue that processes similar to those studied in laboratories and institutes of research are not a part of the daily life-experience of the young and hence do not come within the scope of education based upon experience. That the immature cannot study scientific facts and principles in the way in which mature experts study them goes without saying. But this fact, instead of exempting the educator from responsibility for using present experiences so that learners may gradually be led, through extraction of facts and laws, to experience of a scientific order, sets one of his main problems.

For if it is true that existing experience in detail and also on a wide scale is what it is because of the application of science, first, to processes of production and distribution of goods and services, and then to the relations which human beings sustain socially to one another, it is impossible to obtain an understanding of present social forces (without which they cannot be mastered and directed) apart from an education which leads learners into knowledge of the very same facts and principles which in their final organization constitute the sciences. Nor does the importance of the principle that learners should be led to acquaintance with scientific subject-matter cease with the insight thereby given into present social issues. The methods of science also point the way to the measures and policies by means of which a better social order can be brought into existence. The applications of science which have produced in large measure the social conditions which now exist do not exhaust the possible field of their application. For so far science has been applied more or less casually and under the influence of ends, such as private advantage and power, which are a heritage from the institutions of a prescientific age.

2

Ideals of Man's Nature

INTRODUCTION

In Chapter 1 Plato and Dewey focused on the ideal of citizenship, considering how education might serve the ideal. Now the argument changes, with Hutchins and Maritain propounding ideals of man's nature and the potential of education to serve in the development of rational and spiritual perfection. The challenge in this chapter is provided by Hook and Dewey.

Hutchins provides a suitable link with the preceding discussions, for some of his arguments clash headlong with Dewey's and support Plato's, as though the dialogue were continuing backward and forward across the centuries. Hutchins disagrees with Dewey's notions of the close connections between experience and education. Young people can learn from experience when they leave college, he says. The primary task of formal education, Hutchins believes, is to develop the intellect, for man is unique among animals by virtue of his gift of reason. But Hutchins draws ever closer to Plato: young people are not to be free to learn what they like, studies are to be imposed on them (those studies which will best nurture their intellects), and when reason is firmly implanted in them it will be as a guardian to each. The means to this end-in-view is a course in the collected wisdom of the ages that "connect man with man" and sustain the great intellectual tradition.

Hutchins' ideal is that of individual rational perfection. His justification for making it the supreme educational end-in-view is simply that education should develop "the elements of our common human nature." In other words, education is properly based on an understanding of the nature of man. It is this point with which Hook now takes issue. It is not that reason, as such, is viewed as unimportant in education, or that the world would not be infinitely more settled in human relations if behavior were generally more rational. Hook's main objection is that the *argument* is untenable. Why not build an educational program on *every* unique aspect of man's nature, such as his practice of committing suicide? Is one to impose an educational program on youth which is based on such a unique practice? More seriously, man experiences emotions. Why should not his education concentrate on such an aspect of his nature? What justification is there, indeed, for referring to any selected attribute as "*the* nature of man?" And what evidence is there for believing that human nature is completely unchanging, always and everywhere the same? Like Dewey, Hook objects to any Platonic attempt to take human nature out of the world of everyday experience where it can be studied objectively.

The controversy between Maritain and Dewey has common ground with that between Hutchins and Hook on this very question of the proper source of educational ends-in-view. Are they to be derived from empirical evidence or from *a priori* canons based on religious belief? Maritain attempts to justify an ideal of spiritual perfection as an absolute end-in-view by using a "philosophical-religious" argument. Like Hutchins, his base is a viewpoint on the nature of man, but he emphasizes not only the supremacy of intellect founded on human uniqueness in reason, but also man's personal relationship with God. Though his end-in-view is primarily the development of a "human person" toward the ideal of spiritual perfection, a secondary end-in-view is the transmission and preservation of the "spiritual heritage" of the centuries. Those who do not share his premises may feel impelled to accuse Maritain of making metaphysical statements that close the door to rational discussion. Thus, when he asserts that his viewpoint is not supported by sense-experience, but nevertheless "has criteria and proofs of its own" (relating to what is "essential" in man), the effect is to take the discussion out of the natural world which is common ground to all, regardless of their beliefs.

Dewey is not slow to take up the challenge on behalf of those who confine their educational ends-in-view to the world of everyday experience. He stands opposed to Maritain—though not without intolerance himself—in making three points. (1) The problems of life are not to be resolved by reference to any *a priori* insight into ultimate reality. The only knowledge of value in modifying experience comes from reflection on experience itself. (2) Both the resolution of problems and wide agreement on *how* problems are to be resolved, come from common experience. Absolute philosophers provoke disagreement because of the incompatibility of their exclusive claims to "ultimate truth." (3) In educational philosophy the issue is between those who give precedence to obsolete traditions and those who appreciate what can be done by science and scientific method to solve fundamental problems of individual-social relations.

More generally, Maritain and Dewey stand apart in two respects. First, Maritain has an ultimate end-in-view for education, an ideal that lies beyond education itself and even beyond life. It is *extrinsic* to the educational process. Dewey's educational ends-in-view are entirely *intrinsic* to the educational process. Second, Maritain proceeds from truth to experience. Thinking begins with insight, and in his view trust in the absolute truth revealed by insight properly precedes action. Dewey reverses the process. For him, experience leads to truth—a truth that is tentative, modifiable, never absolute. One literally learns from experience.

An Ideal of Rational Perfection

R. M. Hutchins: General Education[1]

One purpose of education is to draw out the elements of our common human nature. These elements are the same in any time or place. The notion of educating a man to live in any particular time or place, to adjust him to any particular environment, is therefore foreign to a true conception of education.

Education implies teaching. Teaching implies knowledge. Knowledge is truth. The truth is everywhere the same.[2] Hence education should be everywhere the same. I do not overlook the possibilities of differences in organization, in administration, in local habits and customs. These are details. I suggest that the heart of any course of study designed for the whole people will be, if education is rightly understood, the same at any time, in any place, under any political, social, or economic conditions. Even the administrative details are likely to be similar because all societies have generic similarity.

If education is rightly understood, it will be understood as the cultivation of the intellect. The cultivation of the intellect is the same good for all men in all societies. It is, moreover, the good for which all other goods are only means. Material prosperity, peace and civil order, justice and the moral virtues are means to the cultivation of the intellect. So Aristotle says in the *Politics:* "Now, in men reason and mind are the end towards which nature strives, so that the generation and moral discipline of the citizens ought to be ordered with a view to them." An education which served the means rather than their end would be misguided.

I agree, of course, that any plan of general education must be such as to educate the student for intelligent action. It must, therefore, start him on the road toward practical wisdom. But the question is what is the best way for education to start him and how far can it carry him. Prudence or practical wisdom selects the means toward the ends that we desire. It is acquired partly from intellectual operations and partly from experience. But the chief requirement for it is correctness in thinking. Since education cannot duplicate the experiences which the student will have when he graduates, it should devote itself to develop-

---

[1] From R. M. Hutchins, *The Higher Learning in America.* New Haven: Yale University Press, 1936, pp. 66-73, with omissions. Reprinted by permission of the Yale University Press.

[2] "It is therefore evident that, as regards the general principles whether of speculative or practical reason, truth or rectitude is the same for all, and is equally known by all." *Summa Theologica,* Part II, Q. 94, Art. 4.

ing correctness in thinking as a means to practical wisdom, that is, to intelligent action.

As Aristotle put it in the *Ethics*, ". . . while young men become geometricians and mathematicians and wise in matters like these, it is thought that a young man of practical wisdom cannot be found. The cause is that such wisdom is concerned not only with universals, but with particulars, but a young man has no experience, for it is length of time that gives experience." Since practical wisdom is "a true and reasoned capacity to act with regard to the things that are good or bad for man," it would seem that education can make its best contribution to the development of practical wisdom by concentrating on the reasoning essential to it.

A modern heresy is that all education is formal education and that formal education must assume the total responsibility for the full development of the individual. The Greek notion that the city educates the man has been forgotten. Everything that educated the man in the city has to be imported into our schools, colleges, and universities. We are beginning to behave as though the home, the church, the state, the newspaper, the radio, the movies, the neighborhood club, and the boy next door did not exist. All the experience that is daily and hourly acquired from these sources is overlooked, and we set out to supply imitations of it in educational institutions. The experience once provided by some of these agencies may be attenuated now; but it would be a bold man who would assert that the young person today lived a life less full of experience than the youth of yesterday. Today as yesterday we may leave experience to other institutions and influences and emphasize in education the contribution that it is supremely fitted to make, the intellectual training of the young. The life they lead when they are out of our hands will give them experience enough. We cannot try to give it to them and at the same time perform the task that is ours and ours alone.

Young people do not spend all their time in school. Their elders commonly spend none of it there. Yet their elders are, we hope, constantly growing in practical wisdom. They are, at least, having experience. If we can teach them while they are being educated how to reason, they may be able to comprehend and assimilate their experience. It is a good principle of educational administration that a college or university should do nothing that another agency can do as well. This is a good principle because a college or university has a vast and complicated job if it does what only it can do. In general education, therefore, we may wisely leave experience to life and set about our job of intellectual training.

If there are permanent studies which every person who wishes to call himself educated should master; if those studies constitute our intellectual inheritance, then those studies should be the center of a general education. They cannot be ignored because they are difficult, or unpleasant, or because they are almost totally missing from our curriculum today. The child-centered school may be attractive to the child, and no doubt is useful as a place in which the little ones may release their inhibitions and hence behave better at home. But educators cannot permit the students to dictate the course of study unless they are prepared to confess that they are nothing but chaperons, supervising an aimless, trial-and-error process which is chiefly valuable because it keeps young people from doing something worse. The free elective system as Mr. Eliot introduced it at Harvard and as Progressive Education adapted it to lower age levels amounted to a denial that there was content to education. Since there was no content to education, we might as well let students follow their own bent. They would at least be interested and pleased and would be as well educated as if they had pursued a prescribed course of study. This overlooks the fact that the aim of education is to connect man with man, to connect the present with the past, and to advance the thinking of the race. If this is the aim of education, it cannot be left to the sporadic, spontaneous interests of children or even of undergraduates.[3]

Mr. Gladstone once remarked that it is difficult to discern the true dimensions of objects in that mirage which covers the studies of one's youth. Even at stages beyond general education, when the student because he has had a general education and because he is more mature might be given wider latitude in selecting the subjects interesting to him, this can be permitted only to a limited degree. If there are an intellectual tradition and an intellectual inheritance in the law, for example, law schools must see to it that they are transmitted to law students even if law students are more interested in the latest devices for evading the Sherman Antitrust Act.

It cannot be assumed that students at any age will always select the subjects that constitute education. If we permit them to avoid them, we cannot confer upon them insignia which certify to the public that

---

[3] Plato, *Republic*, Book IX: " 'And it is plain,' I said, 'that this is the purpose of the law, which is the ally of all classes in the state, and this is the aim of our control of children, our not leaving them free before we have established, so to speak, a constitutional government within them and, by fostering the best element in them with the aid of the like in ourselves, have set up in its place a similar guardian and ruler in the child, and then, and then only we leave it free.' "

they are in our opinion educated. In any field the permanent studies on which the whole development of the subject rests must be mastered if the student is to be educated.

The variations that should be encouraged fall not in the realm of content but in that of method. Allowances for individual differences should be provided for by abolishing all requirements except the examinations and permitting the students to take them whenever in his opinion he is ready to do so. The cultivation of independent thought and study, now almost wholly missing from our program, may thus be somewhat advanced. And this may be done without sacrificing the content of education to the obsessions of the hour or the caprices of the young.

If we are educators we must have a subject matter, and a rational, defensible one. If that subject matter is education, we cannot alter it to suit the whims of parents, students, or the public. Whewell, Master of Trinity College, Cambridge, one hundred years ago, said:

> Young persons may be so employed and so treated, that their caprice, their self-will, their individual tastes and propensities, are educed and developed; but this is not Education. It is not the Education of a Man; for what is educed is not what belongs to man as man, and connects man with man. It is not the Education of a man's Humanity, but the Indulgence of his Individuality

In general education we are interested in drawing out the elements of our common human nature; we are interested in the attributes of the race, not the accidents of individuals.

Sidney Hook: The Nature of Man[1]

> *"They say that habit is second nature.*
> *Who knows but that nature is first*
> *habit?"* PASCAL

We have been attempting to justify the ends of education by their consequences in experience. There is another approach which rules out all reference to consequences as irrelevant. This declares that we are dealing with a metaphysical question, which requires an answer based on the true metaphysics. Its chief exponents in America are Robert M. Hutchins, Monsignor Fulton Sheen, and Mortimer Adler. They hold that the appropriate end of education can be *deduced* from the true nature of man. The true nature of man is that which differentiates him

[1] From Sidney Hook, *Education for Modern Man.* New York: Alfred A. Knopf, Inc., 1963 edition, pp. 68-72. Copyright 1946, 1963 by S. Hook. Reprinted by permission of Alfred A. Knopf, Inc.

from animals, on the one hand, and angels, on the other. It is expressed in the proposition: "Man is a rational animal." From which it is inferred that the end of human education should be the cultivation of reason.

We shall have occasion to see that the term "reason" does not mean the same thing as the term "intelligence"—that it designates something that has a different origin, nature, and function. But for present purposes, we shall ignore the differences in the meanings of the terms "reason" and "intelligence." The main point is that a patent fallacy is involved in the presumed deduction of the ends of education from what uniquely differentiates man from other animals.

First of all, if what we have previously said is true, from what man *is* we can at best reach conclusions only about what human education is, not what it *should be.* What man should be is undoubtedly related to what he is, for no man should be what he cannot be. Yet a proposition about what he is no more uniquely entails what he should be than the recognition of the nature of an egg necessitates our concluding that the egg should become a chicken rather than an egg sandwich.

A further assumption of the argument is the Aristotelian doctrine that the good of anything is the performance of its specific virtue or the realization of its potentiality. The "good" egg is one that becomes a chicken, the "good" man is one who realizes his natural capacity to think. This overlooks the fact that the natural capacities of a thing limit the range of its fulfillments but do not determine any specific fulfillment. Not every natural power of man has only one natural end; and not every power which has one end achieves it by one mode of development. Thinking is no more or no less natural to man than eating and singing. But what, when, and how a man should eat; what, when, and how a man should sing; about what and when he should think—all this depends not so much upon the natural powers of eating, singing, or thinking as upon an ideal of fitness, appropriateness, or goodness, that is *not* given with natural powers but brought to bear *upon* them in social, historical, and personal experience. When we assert that men *should* be rational, we are not talking biology or metaphysics but voicing a social directive that selectively modifies the natural exercise of human powers in the light of preferred consequences among possible alternate uses.

Second, granted for the sake of the argument that animals other than man are incapable of any rationality. The question is an old and difficult one, handled satirically by Plutarch and experimentally by Köhler, both of whom disagree with the airy dogmatism of the neo-Thomists. Nonetheless, rationality is not the only feature which differentiates man from other animals. Man can be defined, and has been by Benjamin Franklin and Karl Marx, as a "tool-making animal." By the same reasoning employed by neo-Thomists, we can "deduce" that man's proper education should be vocational! Man is also the only animal that can will to commit suicide. Does it follow that education should therefore be a preparation for death? Man is also the only animal that ruts all year round. What educational corollary does this unique trait entail?

Thirdly, even if man is a rational animal, he is not only that. He has many other traits—needs, feelings, emotions, desires, whose nobility or ignobility depend upon their social context. An education appropriate to man would not necessarily limit itself to one aspect of his nature even if that aspect were regarded as more valuable than any other. It is a queer view of the nature of any organism that limits itself to a concern only with its differentia. The notion that the education of reason can or should be carried out independently of the education of the emotions has been called by Whitehead "one of the most fatal, erroneous and dangerous conceptions ever introduced into the theory of education."[2] At any rate what is clear is that we can go from the nature of man to the conclusion that we should educate for reason only because some selective principle has been introduced. The basic educational issues, like the basic ethical issues, pose problems of choice. The nature of man is always relevant; but just as relevant is our decision as to what we want to make of it, what we want men to become. At this point no metaphysical deduction, whether proceeding from materialistic or spiritualistic premises concerning the nature of "reality," can guide us.

What, after all, is meant by *"the* nature of man" whenever we speak of relating educational ends to it? The phrase masks a certain ambiguity that makes it difficult to tell whether its reference is empirical or metaphysical. A great deal of philosophical profundity consists in shifting back and forth between these two references and not being found out. When the neo-Thomists speak of *the* nature of man as a basis for educational ideals, their concern is not primarily with biological, psychological, historical, and social features of human behavior. For since these items designate specific processes of *interaction* between an organism and its environment, it would be risky to choose any set of traits as fixing forever *the* nature of human nature, and therefore *the* nature of education. But the position we are examining is concerned precisely with a conception of human nature which will permit the deduction that, in the words of Mr. Hutchins, "education should everywhere be the same." Everywhere and at every time? Everywhere and at every time. In a

---

[2] Alfred North Whitehead: *The Aims of Education and Other Essays* (New York: The Macmillan Company; 1929), p. 9.

weakened form, Mr. Adler repeats this: "If man is a rational animal, constant in nature through history, there must be certain constant features in every sound educational program regardless of culture and epoch."[3] And Mr. Mark van Doren, who carries all of his teacher's ideas to recognizable absurdity, adds that because education and democracy have the same end—the making of men—they are one and the same. "So education is democracy and democracy is education."[4] From man's nature we can apparently deduce not only that education should everywhere be the same, but the social system, too.

If education is determined by human nature, may not human nature change, and with it the nature of education? *"We must insist,"* writes Mr. Hutchins, *"that no matter how environments differ human nature is, always has been, and always will be the same everywhere."*[5]

This is truly a remarkable assertion. Before we inquire on what evidence Mr. Hutchins knows this to be true, let us see what it implies. For one thing, it implies that human nature is completely independent of changes in the world of physical nature with which the human organism is in constant interaction. Now, certainly, Mr. Hutchins cannot know that the world of nature "is, always has been, and always will be the same everywhere." He therefore must believe that no transformation of the physical basis of human life can possibly affect human nature. His assertion further implies that man's nature is completely independent of changes in the human body, particularly the brain and nervous system. At one stroke this calls into question the whole evolutionary approach to the origin and development of the human species. Finally, it implies that the habitation of man's nature in a human body is unaffected by changes in society and social nurture. The enormous range of variation in social behavior, which testifies to the plasticity of the simplest physiological response under cultural conditioning, leaves the essence of human nature unaltered. In short, human nature is taken out of the world altogether. It is removed from any verifiable context in experience which would permit us to identify it and observe its operations. For anything which operates in the world does so in *interaction* with other things that help shape its character.

[3] Mortimer Adler: "The Crisis in Contemporary Education," *Social Frontier,*
     Vol. 5, No. 42 (February 1939), p. 140.
[4] Mark van Doren: *Liberal Education* (New York: Henry Holt & Company;
     1943), p. 38.
[5] Robert M. Hutchins. "Towards a Durable Society," *Fortune,* Vol. 27, No. 6
     (June 1943), p. 158. My italics.

An Ideal of Spiritual Perfection

J. Maritain: The Aims of Education[1]

Man is not merely an animal of nature, like a skylark or a bear. He is also an animal of culture, whose race can subsist only within the development of society and civilization. He is a *historical* animal: hence the multiplicity of cultural or ethico-historical patterns into which man is diversified; hence, too, the essential importance of education. Due to the very fact that he is endowed with a knowing power which is unlimited and which nonetheless only advances step by step, man cannot progress in his own specific life, both intellectually and morally, without being helped by collective experience previously accumulated and preserved, and by a regular transmission of acquired knowledge. In order to reach self-determination, for which he is made, he needs discipline and tradition, which will both weigh heavily on him and strengthen him so as to enable him to struggle against them—which will enrich that very tradition—and the enriched tradition will make possible new struggles, and so forth.

The First Misconception: a Disregard of Ends

Education is an art, and an especially difficult one. Yet it belongs by its nature to the sphere of ethics and practical wisdom. Education is an *ethical* art (or rather a practical wisdom in which a determinate art is embodied). Now every art is a dynamic trend toward an object to be achieved, which is the aim of this art. There is no art without ends; art's very vitality is the energy with which it tends toward its end, without stopping at any intermediary step.

Here we see from the outset the two most general misconceptions against which education must guard itself. The first misconception is a lack or disregard of ends. If means are liked and cultivated for the sake of their own perfection, and not as means alone, to that very extent they cease to lead to the end, and art loses its practicality; its vital efficiency is replaced by a process of infinite multiplication, each means developing and spreading for its own sake. This supremacy of means over end and the consequent collapse of all sure purpose and real efficiency seem to be the main reproach to contemporary education. The means are not bad. On the contrary, they are generally much better than those of the

[1] From J. Maritain, *Education at the Crossroads.* New Haven: Yale University Press, 1943, pp. 2-8, 12-15, with omissions. Reprinted by permission of the Yale University Press.

old pedagogy. The misfortune is precisely that they are so good that we lose sight of the end. Hence the surprising weakness of education today, which proceeds from our attachment to the very perfection of our modern educational means and methods and our failure to bend them toward the end. The child is so well tested and observed, his needs so well detailed, his psychology so clearly cut out, the methods for making it easy for him everywhere so perfected, that the end of all these commendable improvements runs the risk of being forgotten or disregarded. Thus modern medicine is often hampered by the very excellence of its means: for instance, when a doctor makes the examination of the patient's reactions so perfectly and carefully in his laboratory that he forgets the cure; in the meantime the patient may die, for having been too well tended, or rather analyzed. The scientific improvement of the pedagogical means and methods is in itself outstanding progress. But the more it takes on importance, the more it requires a parallel strengthening of practical wisdom and of the dynamic trend toward the goal.

The Second Misconception: False Ideas concerning the End

The second general error or misconception of education does not consist of an actual dearth of appreciation of the end but false or incomplete ideas concerning the nature of this end. The educational task is both greater and more mysterious and, in a sense, humbler than many imagine. If the aim of education is the helping and guiding of man toward his own human achievement, education cannot escape the problems and entanglements of philosophy, for it supposes by its very nature a philosophy of man, and from the outset it is obliged to answer the question: "What is man?" which the philosophical sphinx is asking.

The Scientific and the Philosophical-Religious Idea of Man

I should like to observe at this point that, definitely speaking, there are only two classes or categories of notions concerning man which play fair, so to speak: the purely scientific idea of man and the philosophical-religious one. According to its genuine methodological type, the scientific idea of man, like every idea recast by strictly experimental science, gets rid as far as possible of any ontological content, so that it may be entirely verifiable in sense-experience. On this point the most recent theorists of science, the neopositivists of the school of Vienna, are quite right. The purely scientific idea of man tends only to link together measurable and observable data taken as such, and is determined from the very start not to consider anything like being or essence, not to answer any question like: Is there a soul or isn't there? Does the spirit exist or only matter? Is there freedom or determinism? Purpose or chance? Value or simple fact? For such questions are out of the realm of science. The purely scientific idea of man is, and must be, a phenomenalized idea without reference to ultimate reality.

The philosophical-religious idea of man, on the contrary, is an ontological idea. It is not entirely verifiable in sense-experience, though it possesses criteria and proofs of its own, and it deals with the essential and intrinsic, though not visible or tangible characters, and with the intelligible density of that being which we call man.

Now it is obvious that the purely scientific idea of man can provide us with invaluable and ever-growing information concerning the means and tools of education, but by itself it can neither primarily found nor primarily guide education, for education needs primarily to know what man *is*, what is the nature of man and the scale of values it essentially involves; and the purely scientific idea of man, because it ignores "being-as-such," does not know such things, but only what emerges from the human being in the realm of sense observation and measurement. Young Tom, Dick, or Harry, who are the subjects of education, are not only a set of physical, biological, and psychological phenomena, the knowledge of which is moreover thoroughly needed and necessary; they are the children of man—this very name "man" designating for the common sense of parents, educators, and society the same ontological mystery as is recognized in the rational knowledge of philosophers and theologians.

It should be pointed out that if we tried to build education on the single pattern of the scientific idea of man and carry it out accordingly, we could only do so by distorting or warping this idea: for we should have to ask what is the nature and destiny of man, and we should be pressing the only idea at our disposal, that is the scientific one, for an answer to our question. Then we would try, contrary to its type, to draw from it a kind of metaphysics. From the logical point of view, we would have a spurious metaphysics disguised as science and yet deprived of any really philosophical insight; and from the practical point of view, we would have a denial or misconception of those very realities and values without which education loses all human sense or becomes the training of an animal for the utility of the state.

Thus the fact remains that the complete and integral idea of man which is the prerequisite of education can only be a philosophical and religious idea of man. I say philosophical, because this idea pertains to the nature or essence of man; I say religious, because of the existential status of this human nature in relation to God and the special gifts and trials and vocation involved.

The Christian Idea of Man

There are many forms of the philosophical and religious idea of man. When I state that the education of man, in order to be completely well grounded, must be based upon the Christian idea of man, it is because I think that this idea of man is the true one, not because I see our civilization actually permeated with this idea. Yet, for all that, the man of our civilization *is* the Christian man, more or less secularized. Consequently we may accept this idea as a common basis and imply that it is to be agreed upon by the common consciousness in our civilized countries, except among those who adhere to utterly opposite outlooks, like materialistic metaphysics, positivism, or skepticism—I am not speaking here of Fascist and racist creeds, which do not belong at all in the civilized world.

Now such a kind of agreement is all that any doctrine in moral philosophy can be expected to have, for none can pretend actually to obtain the literal universal assent of all minds—not because of any weakness in objective proof but because of the weakness inherent in human minds.

There does exist, indeed, among the diverse great metaphysical outlooks, if they recognize the dignity of the spirit, and among the diverse forms of Christian creeds, or even of religious creeds in general, if they recognize the divine destiny of man, a community of analogy as concerns practical attitudes and the realm of action, which makes possible a genuine human coöperation. In a Judeo-Greco-Christian civilization like ours, this community of analogy, which extends from the most orthodox religious forms of thought to the mere humanistic ones, makes it possible for a Christian philosophy of education, if it is well founded and rationally developed, to play an inspiring part in the concert, even for those who do not share in the creed of its supporters. Be it added, by the way, that the term concert, which I just used, seems rather euphemistic with regard to our "modern philosophies of education," whose discordant voices have been so valuably studied in Professor Brubacher's book.[2]

In answer to our question, then, "What is man?" we may give the Greek, Jewish, and Christian idea of man: man as an animal endowed with reason, whose supreme dignity is in the intellect; and man as a free individual in personal relation with God, whose supreme righteousness consists in voluntary obeying the law of God; and man as a

[2] Cf. John S. Brubacher, *Modern Philosophies of Education* (New York and London, 1939).

sinful and wounded creature called to divine life and to the freedom of grace, whose supreme perfection consists of love.

Human Personality

From the philosophical point of view alone the main concept to be stressed here is the concept of human personality. Man is a person, who holds himself in hand by his intelligence and his will. He does not merely exist as a physical being. There is in him a richer and nobler existence; he has spiritual superexistence through knowledge and love.

* * * *

... What is of most importance in educators themselves is a respect for the soul as well as for the body of the child, the sense of his innermost essence and his internal resources, and a sort of sacred and loving attention to his mysterious identity, which is a hidden thing that no techniques can reach.

* * * *

The Third Misconception: Pragmatism

... We find ourselves confronted with the inappropriateness of the pragmatic overemphasis in education—a third error or misconception that we meet on our path. Many things are excellent in the emphasis on action and "praxis," for life consists of action. But action and praxis aim at an object, a determining end without which they lose direction and vitality. And life exists, too, for an end which makes it worthy of being lived. Contemplation and self-perfection, in which human life aspires to flower forth, escape the purview of the pragmatic mind.

It is an unfortunate mistake to define human thought as an organ of response to the actual stimuli and situations of the environment, that is to say, to define it in terms of animal knowledge and reaction, for such a definition exactly covers the way of "thinking" proper only to animals without reason. On the contrary, it is because every human idea, to have a meaning, must attain in some measure (be it even in the symbols of a mathematical interpretation of phenomena), what things *are* or consist of unto themselves; it is because human thought is an instrument or rather a vital energy of knowledge or spiritual intuition (I don't mean "knowledge about," I mean "knowledge into"); it is because thinking begins, not only with difficulties but with *insights,* and ends up in insights which are made true by rational proving or experimental verifying, not by pragmatic sanction, that human thought is able to illumine experience, to realize desires which are human because they are rooted in the prime desire for unlimited goods, and to dominate, control, and refashion the world. At the beginning of human action, insofar as it is human, there is truth, grasped or believed to be grasped for the sake of truth. Without trust in truth, there is no human effectiveness. Such is, to my mind, the chief criticism to be made of the pragmatic and instrumentalist theory of knowledge.

In the field of education, this pragmatic theory of knowledge, passing from philosophy to upbringing, can hardly produce in the youth anything but a scholarly skepticism equipped with the best techniques of mental training and the best scientific methods, which will be unnaturally used against the very grain of intelligence, so as to cause minds to distrust the very idea of truth and wisdom, and to give up any hope of inner dynamic unity.[3]

*　　*　　*　　*

We may now define in a more precise manner the aim of education. It is to guide man in the evolving dynamism through which he shapes himself as a human person—armed with knowledge, strength of judgment, and moral virtues—while at the same time conveying to him the spiritual heritage of the nation and the civilization in which he is involved, and preserving in this way the century-old achievements of generations.

John Dewey: Ultimate Values or Aims[1]

Philosophy is frequently presented as the systematic endeavor to obtain knowledge of what is called Ultimate and Eternal Reality. Many thinkers have defended this conception of its task and aim on the ground that human life can derive stable guidance only by means of ideals and standards that have their source in Ultimate Reality. On the other hand, scepticism about the worth of philosophy usually rests upon denial of the possibility of attaining such knowledge. When the business of philosophy is conceived in this manner, philosophical oppositions and controversies are believed to spring from conflicting conceptions of the nature of Ultimate and Perfect Reality. One school holds that it is spiritual; another that it is material. One school of thought holds that the

---

[3] The "four cults"—skepticism, presentism, scientism, anti-intellectualism—listed by Dr. Hutchins (*Education for Freedom* [1943], p. 35-36) are but offsprings of pragmatism's domination over education.

[1] From John Dewey, "The Determination of Ultimate Values or Aims through Antecedent or A Priori Speculation or through Pragmatic or Empirical Inquiry." In *National Society for the Study of Education, Thirty-seventh Yearbook, Part II.* Bloomington, Ill.: Public School Publishing Co., 1938, pp. 471-473, 475-480, with omissions. Reprinted by permission of the National Society for the Study of Education.

particulars of the Universe are held together only externally by mechanical bonds; another school holds that they are organically united because of common subordination to a final controlling end and purpose that they all serve. Such divisions are inevitable as long as philosophy is defined as knowledge of supreme reality supposed to be beyond and beneath the things of experience.

But there is an alternative conception of philosophy, and the deepest philosophic divisions do not have their origin in a different conception of ultimate reality, but in the conflict between two opposed conceptions of what philosophy is about, its aim and task. According to this alternative view, the work of philosophy is confined to the things of actual experience. Its business is criticism of experience as it exists at a given time and constructive projection of values, which, when acted upon, will render experience more unified, stable, and progressive. Defects and conflicts in experience as it exists demands thoroughgoing criticism of its contents and procedures. This phase of inquiry is not, however, final; criticism does not end with mere intellectual discrimination. It provides the basis for projection of values as yet unrealized, values that are to be translated into ends that move men to action. Philosophy thus conceived does not involve a flight and escape to that which is beyond experience. It is concerned with making the most possible out of experience, personal and social. Everyday homely objects and occupations of everyday life are possessed of potentialities that, under the guidance of deliberate and systematic intelligence, will make life fuller, richer, and more unified.

There are defects and conflicts in abundance in experience as it exists at any time. But they are to be dealt with in terms of experience, not by running away from it. They are a challenge to project, through systematic reflection, a better ordered and more inclusive experience. Systematic endeavor to meet this challenge constitutes the reality of genuine philosophy. The first-mentioned idea of the work of philosophy rests upon distrust of the capacity of experience to generate fundamental values and to direct deliberate effort in behalf of their realization. This distrust involves lack of loyalty to practical intelligence, substituting in its place dependence upon so-called *a priori* intuitions and upon an alleged faculty of pure Reason that grasps absolute non-empirical truth.

Hence, there is a further fundamental difference between the two ideas of the business of philosophy. According to the first-mentioned view, knowledge, provided that it is knowledge of ultimate reality, is the final goal, complete in independence of practical activity. According to the other view, thought and knowledge cannot themselves resolve the discords of existence and life. Even if there were a Reality beyond and behind the things of the experienced world and even if knowledge of it were possible, knowledge would leave the defects and inconsistencies of the world in which we live just what they were before. Only action can change things in the direction of unity and stability. To accomplish this result, action must be directed by leading principles, and such action, as the fruit of reflection upon actual experience, reveals new and as yet unrealized possibilities. The systematic critical work that is philosophy has its constructive phase in projection of values and ends that, by their very constitution, demand application in action and guide the active operations they project.

There is a practical effect of absolute philosophies. But it is that of promoting conflicts and strengthening appeal to external authority as the sole agency for establishing order and unity in experience. Every absolute philosophy must claim to be in exclusive possession of *the* ultimate truth or else go back on its own pretensions. Absolute philosophies cannot tolerate rivals or learn from opposed philosophies. History shows that such philosophies have met with general acknowledgment only when they have had the support of powerful institutions, political and ecclesiastical. Their practical logic calls for external authority to enforce submission and punish heretical deviations. Absolute truth exacts absolute obedience. Recognition of the relation of philosophic ideas to the conditions set by experience furthers, on the contrary, intercommunication, exchange, and interaction. Through these processes differences of belief are modified in the direction of consensus. They are negotiable.

*   *   *   *

The Philosophy of Education

Its Outstanding Importance

The philosophy of education is one phase of philosophy in general. It may be seriously questioned whether it is not the most important single phase of general philosophy. For education, when it is genuinely educational, brings about not only acquisition of knowledge and skills, but it forms also attitudes and dispositions that direct the uses to which acquired information and skill are put. While not as yet the most powerful existing agency in the formation of the disposition of individuals in its active relation to social needs and values, it is the one agency that deals deliberately and intentionally with the practical solution of the basic relations of the individual and the social. Moreover, it has to do with perpetuation of the positive values of inherited culture by embodying them in the dispositions of individuals who are to transmit culture into the future, and also with the creation of attitudes, understanding, and desire that will produce a better future culture. It performs its work in the medium of learning. Hence, the whole philosophic problem of the origin, nature, and function of knowledge is a live issue in education, not just a problem for exercise of intellectual dialectical gymnastics. Indeed, it would be difficult to find a single important problem of general philosophic inquiry that does not come to a burning focus in matters of the determination of the proper subject matter of studies, the choice of methods of teaching, and the problem of the social organization and administration of the schools.

A Typical Problem: The Relation of Scientific Knowledge to Practical Activity

The fact that the fundamental division between different philosophies is set by two opposed conceptions of the aim and business of philosophy suggests that the problem of knowledge, especially scientific knowledge, in its relation to practical activity be chosen for special consideration. The question of which type of philosophy shall control the philosophy of education is one of practical import. With respect to the organization and conduct of education, the issue is virtually whether traditions established in the past, in a pre-scientific age—traditions that have long endured, that have found expression in institutions that affect life most deeply, and that have gathered about themselves intense emotional attachments—or whether science and the scientific method in connection with experience shall exercise fundamental control.

As a force in the conduct of human affairs, scientific method is extremely new; as a force in education, it is even newer. In the latter, as in life generally, it is still a comparatively superficial coating over a thick layer of deposits from ancient customs, social institutions, and habitual outlooks. Science is endured and even highly approved as long as it is confined to providing more effective means for accomplishing results that are in harmony with the inherited scheme of cultural values. It is distrusted and feared when it threatens to influence and to alter the old system of ends, instead of limiting itself to supplying better means for realizing them. The application of science is welcomed, for example, in industrial life as far as new inventions and new technologies for production and distribution of commodities are concerned. But any endeavor to apply science to the reconstruction of human relations in the existing framework of economic and political institutions, any attempt to alter the values, positive and negative, that the existing system produces, is met with suspicion and active hostility. It is even sometimes treated as an effort to undermine the very foundations of social order.

Something of the same sort exists in the field of education. The application of the results of scientific study to change the methods of teaching subjects that have the sanction of scholastic tradition encounters the resistance of inertia. But upon the whole they are gladly adopted as far as they give increased efficiency in the teaching of reading, writing, arithmetic, geography, etc. Attempts to use the newer knowledge of man and of social relations to give changed social direction to all the subjects of school teaching might be condemned as subversive of the established constitution of human relationships.

At this point what has been said about the general relation of science and philosophy applies to the special field of education. Science can examine the relation of cause and effect between established procedures in teaching and the results that follow in the learning by students of these particular subjects. Knowledge of this relation enables techniques to be developed that accomplish better results with less waste of energy, exactly as knowledge of cause and effect in physical and chemical fields is readily convertible into improved techniques for production of material commodities. But critical survey of the value of the consequences to which even the most improved techniques contribute would place the subjects in a wider context of their relationship to present social needs and issues. Improvement of old procedures is a gain. But it does not decide the nature of the ends to which education should contribute nor the right of the studies, even when taught more efficiently, to a place in the course of study. That question can be settled only by consideration of possibilities inherent in the science of social and cultural life—possibilities not adequately represented in the scheme of education that has come to us from traditions that have not been subjected to thoroughgoing criticism.

What has just been said does not imply, however, that there is a sharp separation, a hard-and-fast line of division, between science and philosophy in education. Existing conditions and their effects can be examined scientifically in a sense that unrealized possibilities cannot be. Yet there is a necessary connection between existing conditions and the values and ends that as yet are possible rather than actual. It is true, for example, that while science can determine the most effective ways of producing explosives, it cannot within this limited physical and chemical field determine the ends for which they shall be used; whether for destruction of life and property in war, or for blasting away obstructions to easy communication and providing materials for the better housing of human beings. But an examination of the human consequences of warlike and peaceful pursuits is also possible, and this examination should be carried on in the objective spirit of science. The institution of war is capable of being subjected to critical survey, and critical survey will be intelligent only as it adopts the method of tracing relations of cause and effect that have proved to be effective in attaining knowledge in physical matters. When the effects taken into account are consequences upon human welfare, inquiry has passed into a field that, by comparison, is philosophical, since it has to do with values.

* * * *

It is not . . . an accidental matter that the present-day adherents of absolutistic, super-empirical philosophies base their criticisms of existing education and their proposals of reform upon appeal to Greek and Medieval tradition. For it was in ancient Greece that a philosophy of super-empirical Reality, and of truths about it that are identical under all conditions of experience, was formulated; and it was in the Middle Ages that, because of the sanction and support of a powerful social institution, philosophy actually flourished in the organized constitution of society. The conflict of the two philosophies of education is, therefore, a conflict between the intellectual and moral attitudes of a prescientific past and those consonant with the potentialities of the living present. Insistence upon the necessity of making a sharp separation between liberal and vocational education, upon the importance of literary classics in contrast with scientific subjects (with the exception of mathematics treated as an exemplar of a system of absolute truths instead of as an ordered system of deductions from freely chosen postulates), and lack of faith in anything approaching first-hand experience in the schools, all flow logically from the philosophy that rests upon return to the past. The function of a philosophy of education based upon experience is, on the contrary, constructive exploration of the possibilities of experience directed by scientific method.

For the only way out of existing educational confusion and conflict is just the critical and constructive exploration of the potentialities of existing experience as that experience is brought under the fuller control of intelligence represented by scientific method. The existing school system presents, like existing life and culture, an incoherent mixture of values and standards derived from the old and the new. The school has neither the benefit of values inherent in a culture that existed centuries ago not yet of the values inherent in those possibilities of present experience that can be realized by a more thoroughgoing use of scientific method. On the one hand, schools are so peculiarly subject to the power of tradition and of uncriticized custom that they embody the subjects and ends of the past. On the other hand, pressure of demands arising from existing conditions, especially those arising from contemporary industrial and economic institutions, has compelled the introduction of new subjects and new courses of study. The educational response in the latter case has been, however, almost as uncritical as the response that is exhibited in the adoption of values and ends having the sanction of tradition. Science and the applications of science that ushered in first the machine age and now the age of power have forced by their sheer social pressure the introduction into the educational system of scientific subjects and of occupational training. But to a large extent these new subjects overlay the older ones as a recent geological stratum overlays, with 'faults' and distortions, older deposits.

Part

II

Objectives

3

Simple Objectives

INTRODUCTION

Educational aims assume a strikingly different complexion as one swings from the remotest and most visionary educational ideals considered in Chapter I to the simple objectives represented in this chapter. In the first section the objectives are the simplest and the contrast with ideals is most apparent, for here the objectives are very specific, readily attainable, and much easier to comprehend than some of the concepts previously considered, such as concepts of the State and the nature of man. In the second section the simplicity of the objectives is not as sharply marked, although they are still worlds apart from ideals by virtue of their direct attainability.

The indeterminacy of the concepts "simple" and "complex" has been noted in the general introduction to this anthology, but in the present chapter the problem is faced head-on. Although it is not difficult to find particular illustrations of objectives which one would not hesitate to classify as simple and readily attainable, there are clearly others that belong to a No-Man's-Land between the simple and the complex. One of the difficulties is that the words "simple" and "complex" are sometimes deceptive. What is simple to one person may not be so simple to another, and what is superficially single-stranded may in fact turn out upon examination to be multi-stranded. To *know* a short lyrical poem appears to be a simple enough objective to some people, but it is simple only in certain senses of "know." One may memorize the sounds or the written symbols. One may know the poem as an integrated unit of experience, and one may comprehend every separate suggestion in thought and feeling. One may understand all the technical aspects of rhythm, rhyme, and sound patterns, as well as all the subtle inter-relationship of ideas, sounds, and feelings. One may know all of these in combination, or one may know some of them. To know a line of a poem may be anything but a single, specific objective. To know a single word of a poem may be complex enough to be the subject of an essay.

Another characteristic of the simple objective, apart from the element of indeterminary in its central concept is that it does not always denote a separate termination, for seldom does a simple objective have any value in isolation. Simple objectives usually contribute to more complex ones, and are interrelated in a variety of ways. A teacher may aim at a specific understanding of racial prejudice, for instance, not so much for its own sake as for its effect on more lasting attitudes.

On the question of attainability, however, there is no need for reservations. The selections in this chapter contrast strikingly with the remoteness of unrealizable ideals, and their specificity gives them greater clarity of direction. They are signposts to recognizable and well-routed features, rather than pointers to a promised land. Generally, they leave no scope for disputation, and on that account are able to speak plainly for themselves.

In section 1 the illustrations of simple objectives have been selected for their high degree of specificity, immediacy, and directness. The first set of selections is from Bloom's *Taxonomy*,[1] which attempts a systematic classification of cognitive objectives in education. The book is divided into six major classes, so that the objectives of one class are likely to make use of the objectives of preceding classes. Its purpose is scientific and historical, rather than normative, aiming at the collection, identification, and systematization of a vast number of objectives already used—particularly by educational examiners. It is in the manner of a zoological reconstruction attempting to give skeletal form to a variety of discovered bones. The pieces may appear as inert as a natural history display when viewed as a bare chronicle of past educational plans and practices, but they do serve to illustrate simple examination objectives collated from practical experience.

To give point to the highest degree of specificity in these examina-

[1] B. S. Bloom (ed.), *Taxonomy of Educational Objectives Handbook I: Cognitive Domain.* New York: Longmans, Green and Co., 1956.

tion objectives, and thereby to offer the sharpest contrast with ideals, they are offered in two separate illustrations, the second explicitly and perceptibly less specific than the first. Indeed, it is the first only that is conveniently designated as "Knowledge of Specifics." In an introductory explanation, Bloom informs the reader that he will use "knowledge" in the sense of remembering (either by recognition or by recall), and that his classification of knowledge objectives proceeds "from the specific and relatively concrete types of behaviors to the more complex and abstract ones."[2]

The test of whether Bloom's illustrations of "specifics" fit his idea of concrete and simple "bits of information" is to ask the straight-forward question: Can the teacher know whether or not the objective has been achieved? In the light of this question, one soon realizes that although the majority of Bloom's illustrations are appropriate, some are not, for vagueness sometimes prevents a categorical answer. "Familiarity with a large number of words in their common range of meanings" is an instance of this imprecision.

To throw the specifics into greater relief, the second set of illustrations is from "Knowledge of Ways and Means of Dealing with Specifics." It is apparent that the majority of these items are inappropriate to the test of specificity and that a greater measure of abstractness, imprecision, generality, and ambiguity prevails here than in the first set of knowledge objectives. Yet against the semantic looseness of "a knowledge of acceptable forms of language," one finds the high specificity and clarity of "knowledge of the standard representational devices and symbols in maps and charts" clearly appropriate as conventions, but clearly appropriate also as specifics.

The third illustration of specific simple objectives is concerned with teachers' objectives rather than examiners'. One might expect the ultimate in specificity of educational objectives to be related to short-term classroom activities as embodied in a teacher's lesson notes. His objective may be to give pupils further practice in money sums; to give them an understanding of the concept of famine, or to explain how to make a simple basket. By questioning and observing he may readily ascertain whether or not his lesson objectives have been fulfilled.

When curricular theories relate educational objectives to daily ac-

[2] Ibid., p. 62.

tivities, the objectives are apt to assume a similar character of practicality, clarity, and direct attainability, as they do in the illustrations of Stratemeyer's Real-Life-Situations curriculum. This curriculum identifies situations appropriate to early childhood, youth, and adulthood. The selections illustrated here refer to youth.

As in the case of Bloom's specifics, one finds Stratemeyer's objectives to be mostly unambiguous and single-stranded, but in some cases it would be difficult to answer categorically whether the objective has or has not been fulfilled. For instance, a teacher might be doubtful as to whether roles of group discussion are played *effectively,* or whether a student's "poise, manner, and methods of presentation" are in fact *appropriate* for audience situations.

To sum up, both Bloom and Stratemeyer have succeeded in presenting some of the most specific and concrete of identifiable educational objectives, even though in particular cases the precision expected of specificity may be found wanting. Bloom's objectives are abstracted and analyzed from collected written data with the detachment of an empirical study; Stratemeyer's are plucked directly from the stream of experience in classroom and community, and are therefore both closer to life and more concrete than Bloom's. The differences between the two are largely those of purpose.

The simple objectives of section 2 are similar to those of section 1 in their common attainability. They differ from the simple objectives in the preceding section, however, in two related respects. First, their simplicity is largely in form, rather than in substance. Despite a veneer of specificity they have, in fact, a degree of complexity, and may thus be called transitional because of their affinity with the complex objectives presented in the next chapter. Second, because of this element of complexity, they generally take more time and are more difficult to attain than are more specific simple objectives.

In the first illustration, Dressel and Mayhew focus on critical thinking as one of the most significant of the "persuasive objectives" of general education. Their earlier remark that critical thinking is "more complicated than simple recall and restatement of ideas, facts, and principles," is an indication that this objective is not of the same nature as the knowledge specifics from Bloom's *Taxonomy.* The so-called specifics of Dressel and Mayhew are deduced from a close study of the complexity of the problem-solving operation. The authors' purpose is to illustrate the many-sidedness of critical thinking, *not* to analyze specific simple objectives that might be pursued in isolation. The fact that the objective has a variety of facets does not imply that all the facets are capable of separate fulfillment as specifics. Among the illustrated problem-solving aspects of critical thinking there are three categories of items. The first comprises specific objectives, such as recognition of necessary and sufficient conditions, and the distinction between necessary and probable inferences. The second comprises items that might be broken down into specifics, such as detection of formal logical fallacies, and detection of logical relationships among terms and propositions. The third category, however, inclines distinctly toward a complex ability, or a set of complex abilities, and includes the comprehension of a problem and the ability to interpret and reorder it, to formulate hypotheses and conclusions, and to maintain objectivity.

The second illustration is drawn from "Policies for Education in American Democracy," which incorporates an earlier statement entitled "The Purposes of Education in American Democracy." It claims to have collated all the objectives of American education within its four interrelated categories. Like the preceding illustration, the analysis of one of these—civic responsibility—shows itself to be an elaboration of the various aspects of a complex objective. In fact, the objectives of civic responsibility are further removed from the simple and specific than are those of critical thinking. Although the element of complexity in critical thinking is strongly intellectual in character, an even stronger element of complexity in civic responsibility is predominantly dispositional or attitudinal in character. Indeed, the so-called objectives of understanding social structures and social processes, and of possessing economic literacy, are the only two of the twelve listed that are not simply facets of a complex disposition. None of them is a simple objective. The objective of developing a *sensitivity to* the disparities of human circumstance entails much more than a simple understanding of inequality of opportunity. Similarly, a *respect for* the law entails much more than a simple understanding of the law.

In brief, the objectives of civic responsibility are scarcely separable from their complex matrix. For that very reason they provide an effective link with the complex objectives of Chapter 4.

Specific Simple Objectives

B. S. Bloom: Knowledge of Specifics[1]

The recall of specific and isolable bits of information. This refers primarily to what might be called the hard core of facts or information in each field of knowledge. Such information represents the elements the specialist must use in communicating about his field, in understanding it, and in organizing it systematically. These specifics are usually quite serviceable to people working in the field in the very form in which they are presented and need little or no alteration from one use or application to another. Such specifics also become the basic elements the student or learner must know if he is to be acquainted with the field or to solve any of the problems in it. These specifics usually are symbols which have some concrete referents and are, for the most part, at a relatively low level of abstraction. There is a tremendous wealth of these specifics and there must always be some selection for educational purposes, since it is almost inconceivable that a student can learn all of the specifics relevant to a particular field. As our knowledge in the social sciences, the sciences, and the humanities increases, even the specialist has great difficulty in keeping up with all the new specifics found or developed in the field. For classification purposes, the specifics may be distinguished from the more complex classes of knowledge by virtue of their very specificity, that is, they can be isolated as elements or bits which have some meaning and value by themselves.

Knowledge of terminology

Knowledge of the referents for specific verbal and non-verbal symbols. This may include knowledge of the most generally accepted symbol referent, knowledge of the variety of symbols which may be used for a single referent, or knowledge of the referent most appropriate to a given use of a symbol.

Probably the most basic type of knowledge in a particular field is its terminology. Each field contains a large number of symbols, either verbal or non-verbal, which have particular referents. These represent the basic language of the field—the shorthand used by the workers in a field

---

[1] From B. S. Bloom (ed.), *Taxony of Educational Objectives Handbook I: Cognitive Domain.* New York: Longmans, Green and Co., 1956, pp. 63-67, 69-71, with omissions. Reprinted by permission of David McKay Company, Inc.

to express what they know. In any attempt by workers to communicate with others about phenomena within the field, they find it necessary to make use of some of the special symbols and terms they have devised. In many cases it is impossible for them to discuss problems in their field without making use of some of the essential terms of that field. Quite literally, they are unable to even think about many of the phenomena in the field unless they make use of these terms and symbols. The learner must become cognizant of these terms and symbols and must learn the generally accepted definitions or meanings to be attached. Just as the specialist in the field must communicate by the use of these terms, so the learner or the individual reader of the communication must have a knowledge of the symbols and their referents before he can comprehend or think about the phenomena of the field.

Here, to a larger extent than in any of the other classes of knowledge objectives, there is a likelihood that the specialist, finding his own symbols useful and precise, will attempt to impose upon the learner a larger number of the symbols than the learner really needs, can learn, or will retain. Especially is this true in many of the sciences which attempt to use words and symbols with great precision and where the specialist finds it difficult to express the same ideas or discuss particular phenomena by the use of other symbols or by the use of other terms much more common to a lay population.

Knowledge of Terminology—Illustrative Educational Objectives

To define technical terms by giving their attributes, properties, or relations.

The ability to distinguish the referents for words and to establish the limits within which a biological term may have meaning.

Familiarity with a large number of words in their common range of meanings.

Knowledge of the vocabulary of the fine arts sufficient to be able to read and converse intelligently.

To acquire an understanding of the vocabulary used in quantitative thinking.

Knowledge of the terms and concepts peculiar to work in science.

Knowledge of important accounting terms.

Mastery of the terms peculiar to work in science.

To acquire an understanding of the terminology associated with geometric figures on a plane.

Knowledge of Specific Facts

Knowledge of dates, events, persons, places, sources of information, etc.
This may include very precise and specific information, such as the exact
date of an event or the exact magnitude of a phenomenon. It may also
include approximate information, such as a time period in which an
event occurred or the general order of magnitude of a phenomenon.
Knowledge of specific facts refers to those facts which can be isolated
as separate, discrete elements in contrast to those which can only be
known in a larger context.

In every field there are a large number of dates, events, persons,
places, findings, etc., known by the specialist which represent findings or
knowledge about the field. These can be distinguished from the terminology in that the terminology generally represents the conventions or
agreements within a field, while the facts are more likely to represent
the findings which can be tested by other means than determining the
unanimity of workers in the field or the agreements they have made for
purposes of communication. Such specific facts also represent basic elements which the specialist must use in presenting communications about
the field and in thinking about specific problems or topics in the field.
It should also be recognized that this classification includes knowledge
about particular books, writing, and sources of information on specific
topics and problems. Thus, knowledge of a specific fact as well as knowledge of the source which deals with the fact are both classifiable under
this heading.

Again, there is usually a tremendous number of such specific facts
and the teacher or curriculum specialist must make choices as to what is
basic and what is only of secondary importance or of importance primarily to the specialist. The teacher is also confronted with the problem
of level of precision with which different information must be known.
Thus, quite frequently he may be content to have a student learn only
the approximate magnitude of the phenomenon rather than its precise
quantity or to learn an approximate time period rather than the precise
date or time of a specific event. The teacher also has a considerable
problem in determining whether many of the specific facts are such
that the student can learn them whenever he really needs them, or
whether they should be learned during and as part of an educational
unit or course.

Knowledge of Specific Facts—Illustrative Educational Objectives

The recall of major facts about particular cultures.

The possession of a minimum knowledge about the organisms studied in the laboratory.

Knowledge of biological facts important to a systematic understanding of biological processes.

Recall and recognition of factual information about contemporary society.

Knowledge of practical biological facts important to health, citizenship, and other human needs.

Acquiring information about major natural resources.

Acquiring information about various important aspects of nutrition.

Recall and recognition of what is characteristic of particular periods.

Knowledge of physical and chemical properties of common elements and their compounds.

An acquaintance with the more significant names, places, and events in the news.

A knowledge of the reputation of a given author for presenting and interpreting facts on governmental problems.

Knowledge of reliable sources of information for wise purchasing.

Knowledge of Ways and Means of Dealing With Specifics

Knowledge of Conventions

Knowledge of characteristic ways of treating and presenting ideas and phenomena. These are the usages, styles, and practices which are employed in a field because the workers find they suit their purposes or because they appear to suit the phenomena with which they deal. This may include such varied phenomena as conventional symbols used in map making and dictionaries, rules of social behavior, and rules, styles, or practices commonly employed in scholarly fields.

There are many conventions and rules which the workers in a field find extremely useful in dealing with the phenomena of a field. Although many such conventions may be retained because of habit and tradition rather than usefulness, at some point in time they were found to be especially significant in giving some structure to the phenomena. Generally these conventions will have an arbitrary existence since they were developed or retained because of general agreement or concurrence of workers in the field. They are usually true only as a matter of definition and practice rather than as a result of discovery or observation.

In some fields these conventions make up the largest proportion of the knowledge of the field. It is likely that students are more willing to accept and learn this type of knowledge in the early school years than in the later years of formal education.

Knowledge of Conventions—Illustrative Educational Objectives

Familiarity with the forms and conventions of the major types of works, e.g., verse, plays, scientific papers, etc.

To make pupils conscious of correct form and usage in speech and writing.

Knowledge of common rules of etiquette.

To develop a knowledge of acceptable forms of language.

Knowledge of the ways in which symbols are used to indicate the correct pronunciation of words.

Knowledge of the standard representational devices and symbols in maps and charts.

A knowledge of the rules of punctuation.

Knowledge of Trends and Sequences

Knowledge of the processes, directions, and movements of phenomena with respect to time.   It includes trends as attempts to point up the interrelationship among a number of specific events which are separated by time. It also includes representations of processes which may involve time as well as causal interrelations of a series of specific events. Out of an almost infinite number of specific events, particular workers have selected those which they believe point to a trend or sequence. In this respect trends and sequences are those relationships and processes which have been selected or emphasized by the workers in the field. Many of the trends and sequences are difficult to communicate because they involve highly dynamic actions, processes, and movements which are not fully represented by static verbal, graphic, or symbolic forms.

Students may have difficulty in learning trends and sequences unless they are also familiar with the specifics on which such trends and sequences are based.

Knowledge of Trends and Sequences—Illustrative Educational Objectives.

Understanding of the continuity and development of American culture as exemplified in American life.

Knowledge of the basic trends underlying the development of public assistance programs with particular reference to such programs as WPA, PWA, etc., developed during the depression.

Knowledge of trends in government in the United States during the last fifty years.

To develop a basic knowledge of the evolutionary development of man.

To develop a knowledge of effects of industrialization on the culture and international relations of a nation.

To know and describe the forces which determine and shape public policies.

To understand the increasing importance of administrative departments of the national government in formulating public policies.

To know how Greek civilization has affected the contemporary world.

To know how militarism and imperialism have been of causal importance for the world wars.

To develop a knowledge of how hereditary and environmental factors interrelate to influence the development of the individual.

A knowledge of the forces, past and present, which have made for the increasing interdependence of people all over the world.

Florence B. Stratemeyer, *et al.*: Making Things Clear[1]

Extending techniques for participating in a variety of situations involving discussion and conversation. Taking part in class discussions; sharing in student council discussions; acting as discussion chairman; chairing or participating in formal meetings; chairing or actng as panel member; acting as member of debating team; using telephone appropriately for variety of purposes; interviewing school visitors; being interviewed for job; acting as salesman in part-time job; acting as host at class tea, dinner, parties at home; adjusting conversation to varied situations and age levels; acquiring insights into more complex problems of grammatical usage; acquiring techniques needed to play a variety of roles in group discussion effectively; acquiring techniques needed to meet many of these same problems when conversing in another language . . .

Extending ability to use oral presentation effectively for a variety of purposes. Reporting results of research or reading done independyounger children in school; reading minutes of class or council meeting; ently or by committee; taking part in school speakers' bureau; making campaign speeches in school elections; presenting council proposal to

---

[1] From Florence B. Stratemeyer *et al., Developing a Curriculum for Modern Living.* New York: Teachers College Press, 2nd edition, 1957, pp. 195, 197, 243, with omissions. Reprinted by permission of Teachers College Press, Columbia University; copyright 1957.

chairing or participating in all-school assemblies; taking part in a youth service in church; representing school as panel member on television or radio presentation, or at meeting of local organization; telling stories to younger members of family, camp, or church school groups; reading materials aloud effectively for wide variety of purposes; acquiring poise, manner, and methods of presentation appropriate for a variety of audience situations ...

Extending the range and variety of uses of written expression.
Writing more extensive papers or committee reports based on reading; taking notes from a variety of sources to solve problem; outlining in detail plans for a paper or committee report; making an extensive and accurate bibliography; writing friendly and business letters appropriate to wide variety of situations; filling in forms requesting personal data; writing an order, letters of application; developing more effective style in writing stories, poetry; writing announcements, reports, stories for school paper, magazine; acquiring skill with correct forms of usage, manuscript style appropriate for advanced writing problems; using knowledge of grammar and rules of usage to proofread ...

Extending the range of uses and variety of forms of graphic expression.
Illustrating class paper, school magazine; using cartoons to express an opinion; using diagrams to explain a game; preparing appropriate tables, graphs, or charts to express factual data; using murals or friezes to summarize information; using a variety of projections of maps; using film or slides as aids in a presentation; developing more complex time lines or other devices for summarizing related facts; developing bulletin-board displays to advance school projects; planning advertising campaign for school projects; developing increased skill in selecting and using forms of graphic presentation for maximum effectiveness ...

Participating in Social Activities
(Determining Kind of Social Activity)

Developing increased sensitivity to the needs of others in making demands and undertaking obligations. Deciding what personal services to ask of family and when; adjusting requests for use of family property to needs of others—car, television, telephone; determining what responsibilities one has to parents—in sharing household tasks, in informing them about activities, in demands on family funds; deciding what favors to ask of or grant "best" friends—borrowing money, borrowing clothes, help on special jobs; deciding how exclusive a given friendship should be—whether to "go steady" with one person, whether "best" friend should have other close friendships; considering when to ask friends to adjust activities to one's interests, when one should do what friends demand . . .

Gaining increased ability to adjust responses in a variety of casual social situations.   Getting acquainted with new pupils; helping visitors from another school feel at home; visiting with parents of friends; adjusting introduction to particular situation; deciding what special consideration to give to women, to elderly persons, to other adults; acting as host or hostess at school affair; learning how to initiate and carry conversation with persons whom one meets casually . . .

Extending ability to plan social activities appropriate to a variety of situations.   Deciding what activities to plan for a date; determining the number and kind of all-school functions to have during year; deciding what activities at class party will best meet the needs of all; deciding whether to plan class function in which expenses and kind of clothing demanded will bar some members; planning how one's club can entertain another group; helping plan school affair to entertain parents; acting on program committee of club or church youth group; entertaining friends at home . . .

Transitional Simple Objectives

Paul L. Dressel and Lewis B. Mayhew: Critical Thinking[1]

... As a starting point in consideration of critical thinking, it perhaps can be accepted that students—as one result of their educational experience—should be able to carry on types of mental activity more complicated than simple recall and restatement of ideas, facts, principles, etc., given in the textbook or presented by the instructor in his lectures, but this broad conception is useless for either evaluation or instruction.

One of the earliest points of agreement about critical thinking was that it did not include "imaginative thinking," but this negative approach was quickly abandoned for a positive approach involving a listing of critical thinking abilities. For this purpose "problem solving," which was regarded as embracing most of the aspects of critical thinking, was adopted as the ability to be particularized. This restriction was decided upon because of a feeling that problem solving is essential to effective living. A detailed list of problem-solving abilities follows.

A TENTATIVE LIST OF THE PROBLEM-SOLVING ASPECTS OF CRITICAL THINKING

1. *Ability to Recognize the Existence of a Problem*
   a. To recognize related conditions in a situation.
   b. To recognize conflicts and issues in a situation.
   c. To locate "missing links" in a series of ideas or incidents.
   d. To recognize problems which have no solution.

2. *Ability to Define the Problem*
   a. To identify the nature of the problem.
   b. To understand what is involved and required in the problem.
   c. To recognize ways in which the problem can be phrased.
   d. To define difficult and abstract elements of the problem in simple, concrete, and familiar terms.
   e. To break complex elements of the problem into workable parts.
   f. To identify the central elements of the problem.
   g. To place the elements of the problem into an order in which they can be handled.

---

[1] From Paul L. Dressel and Lewis B. Mayhew, *General Education: Explorations in Evaluation.* Washington, D.C.: American Council on Education, 1954, pp. 176-179, with omissions. Reprinted by permission of the American Council on Education.

      h. To eliminate extraneous elements from the problem.

      i. To place the problem in its context.

3. *Ability to Select Information Pertinent to the Solution of the Problem*
    a. To distinguish reliable and unreliable sources of information.
    b. To recognize bias upon which information is selected and rejected.
    c. To recognize information relevant to the solution of the problem.
    d. To select adequate and reliable samples of information.
    e. To systematize information.
    f. To select information from personal experience relevant to the solution of the problem.

4. *Ability to Recognize Assumptions Bearing on the Problem*
    a. To identify unstated assumptions.
    b. To identify unsupported assumptions.
    c. To identify irrelevant assumptions.

5. *Ability to Make Relevant Hypotheses*
    a. To discover clues to the solution of the problem.
    b. To formulate various hypotheses on the basis of information and assumptions.
    c. To select the more promising hypotheses for first consideration.
    d. To check the consistency of the hypotheses with the information and assumptions
    e. To make hypotheses concerning unknown and needed information.

6. *Ability to Draw Conclusions Validly from Assumptions, Hypotheses, and Pertinent Information*
    a. To detect logical relationships among terms and propositions.
    b. To recognize necessary and sufficient conditions.
    c. To identify cause and effect relationships.
    d. To identify and state the conclusion.

7. *Ability to Judge the Validity of the Processes Leading to the Conclusion*
    a. To distinguish validly drawn conclusions from others chosen, for example, because they are in accord with values, preferences, and biases.
    b. To distinguish a necessary inference from a probable one.
    c. To detect formal logical inconsistencies in the argument.

8. *Ability to Evaluate a Conclusion in Terms of Its Application*
    a. To recognize conditions which would be necessary to verify a conclusion.
    b. To recognize conditions which would make a conclusion inapplicable.
    c. To judge the adequacy of a conclusion as a solution of the problem.

The preceding list is only one of many possible. Critical thinking is a complicated mental activity, and an almost endless list of specifics could be produced, no two items of which would be completely inter-dependent. Equally clearly they would not be independent, particularly if an attempt is made to view them as they might be applied in solving a problem. Therefore, this or any other list must be regarded primarily as an aid in understanding the nature of critical thinking, and the specifics of the list must not be allowed to usurp attention to the point where their integration and augmentation by other unlisted abilities into the still undefined complex mental ability—critical thinking—is forgotten.

Education Policies Commission: The Objectives of Civic Responsibility[1]

.... Four aspects of educational purpose have been identified. These aspects center around the person himself, his relationships to others in home and community, the creation and use of material wealth, and socio-civic activities. The first area calls for a description of the educated *person;* the second, for a description of the educated *member of the family and community group;* the third, of the educated *producer or consumer;* the fourth, of the educated *citizen.* The four great groups of objectives thus defined are:

1. The Objectives of Self-Realization
2. The Objectives of Human Relationship
3. The Objectives of Economic Efficiency
4. The Objectives of Civic Responsibility.

Each of these is related to each of the others. Each is capable of further subdivision.

The Objectives of Civic Responsibility

Social Justice. The educated citizen is sensitive to the disparities of human circumstance.

Social Activity. The educated citizen acts to correct unsatisfactory conditions.

Social Understanding. The educated citizen seeks to understand social structures and social processes.

Critical Judgment. The educated citizen has defenses against propaganda.

[1] From the Education Policies Commission, *Policies for Education in American Democracy.* Washington, D.C.: National Education Association of the United States, 1946, pp. 189-190, 240, with omissions. Reprinted by permission of the National Education Association of the United States.

Tolerance. The educated citizen respects honest differences of opinion.

Conservation. The educated citizen has a regard for the nation's resources.

Social Applications of Science. The educated citizen measures scientific advance by its contribution to the general welfare.

World Citizenship. The educated citizen is a cooperating member of the world community.

Law Observance. The educated citizen respects the law.

Economic Literacy. The educated citizen is economically literate.

Political Citizenship. The educated citizen accepts his civic duties.

Devotion to Democracy. The educated citizen acts upon an unswerving loyalty to democratic ideals.

4

Complex Objectives
(Attitudinal Dispositions)

The ends-in-view now grouped as complex objectives are termed "objectives" because of their potential attainability. The justification for describing them as "complex" is best explained by noting their differences from the specific simple objectives of Chapter 3, section 1, which are both simpler in structure, and quicker and easier to attain. The distinction between *intellectual* and *dispositional* complex objectives is not clear-cut, although section 2 of the preceding chapter has suggested that as a complex objective *critical thinking* may be regarded as predominantly intellectual,[1] whereas *civic responsibility* may be regarded as dispositional with a strong affective component. This distinction, however, becomes tenuous on further investigation.

Although "disposition" may refer merely to an *inclination* toward behavior of a certain kind, when used as an educational objective it usually connotes complexity, cohesion, and durability. The closest psychological concept to this connotation is that of attitude,[2] itself a reminder that thought and feeling, intellect and emotion are not strictly separable. By definition, attitudes are complex organizations of thoughts, ideas, or beliefs which are given a degree of cohesion by a necessary component of *feeling:* they have a "stubborn" or lasting quality, they are based on

---

[1] A scientific outlook may be regarded similarily. See P.L. Dressel and L.B. Mayhew, *op.cit.*, pp. 142-143.

[2] See, for example, D. Krech and R.S. Crutchfield, *Elements of Psychology,* 1958, p. 671.

experience and learned from experience, and they shape an individual's response to certain objects in ways that are characteristic of the individual's attitudes. A disposition of civic responsibility may be considered attitudinal in this general sense, with both affective and intellectual components. Although critical thinking and scientific outlook appear on first impressions to be concerned almost solely with intellectual abilities and skills, their involvement with open-mindedness gives them an attitudinal aspect in which the intellectual and affective are inseparable.

What is the justification for focusing in this chapter on dispositions of the attitudinal kind? The answer lies first in their durability and second in their individuality. On the first point, many educators support the formation of attitudes as by far the worthiest of all educational objectives, contrasting them with specific objectives that are apt, once attained, to be quickly lost unless retention is aided by frequent practice. On the second point, although the attitudinal objective is usually formulated externally or publicly by educators, its attainment depends on its assimilation by the learner, and on a transformation of the end-in-view from public to private objective, or goal. A pupil can work through a problem in algebra half-heartedly to satisfy the demands of a teacher, but he cannot be half-hearted if he is to learn a complex disposition. It is contradictory to speak of anyone successfully learning to be tolerant or successfully learning to enjoy an aesthetic experience against his will. In proportion to the degree of personal commitment involved, attitudinal objectives are strongly directive of behavior, and therefore of obvious significance in education. It is by virtue of this self-orientation that they are linked with the private ends-in-view of the following chapter.

The dispositions of this chapter are divided into two sections. In section 1 they seek justification from absolutes; in section 2 they have reference to the empirical world only.

In the first section Buber speaks first, followed by Plato. Although their ideals differ, the contemporary and the ancient have four points in common: (1) each hinges his desired disposition to an absolute; (2) each is strongly normative, urging social unity and harmony; (3) each has a yearning for man's personal unity; and (4) in each the dispositions in mind tend to be obscured by metaphysical statements.

On the question of the absolute, Buber's ideal is akin to Maritain's: a spiritual perfection of man that draws him to the perfection of God.

Plato's ideal man is one who can see reality. He is the philosopher-ruler, alone among mortals for his divine vision of the good (which, although belonging to another world, is the quintessence of reality).

Although Buber and Plato each speak with the background of a society without cohesion or personal trust and responsibility, there is a common plea for social unity. Buber's background is one of modern society where the individual is lost in the mass; Plato's is of a small ancient society that has disintegrated through war, intrigue, and civil strife. Both thinkers search for dispositions that will restore unity to man and to society.

Although centuries apart, each feels the need for harmony and unity in man: man's unity is but one aspect of social unity, his individual harmony and the wider social harmony coalescing. Buber aims to achieve personal unity by education of character. The disposition to be developed is one where the individual has the courage to be himself, to make personal choices, and to accept responsibility for his decisions and his actions. It is a disposition that will enable the individual to stand as an independent human subject against the submerging, objectifying influences of the masses with their powerful pressures toward conformity and anonymity. It is personal integrity that is involved.

Plato is much more interested in social than in personal unity, although he likens the soul of man to the state in their common need for harmony and unity. His main educational theme is that this harmony in man and state alike can be developed by forming dispositions. Since young children are impressionable, stories are to be carefully selected for their beauty and for their absence of every element of civil dissension and family discord. Early impressions are apt to be indelible. From childhood to youth dispositions are formed largely by imitation, and it is therefore imperative that those youths being trained as guardians should be free to imitate only appropriate virtues, such as bravery, temperance, and piety. They are also to be presented with all that is "fair and graceful" in the arts and crafts so that rhythm and harmony may enter "the innermost part of the soul." Music and gymnastics are to be complementary, harmonizing spirit and gentleness. Only those with the noblest dispositions[3] will proceed to the highest study, leading to perception of the good.

[3] *The Republic, op.cit.,* pp. 212, 230.

Over all that is achievable, both Buber and Plato place a veil of mystery and metaphysical irrefutability. Those experiencing the "indefinable unity of a moral destiny" in their "innermost life," Buber attests, are aware of a mystery which they can only contemplate with awe. The unity he seeks is proclaimed as one of the eternal values, serving a divine purpose. Only unified persons can apprehend "the great and full relation between man and man." Plato's reverence for the good as "the cause of all that is right and beautiful in all things—the giver of truth and reason,"[4] is of a similar metaphysical kind.

At this stage a radical counter-position is introduced. Feigl, challenging the views of Buber and Plato, has only one thing in common with them: a normative purpose. Three opposing principles emerge clearly from his article: his forthright rejection of a supernatural world of values, his dedication to empirical and rational methods of inquiry, and a reliance on statements that are examinable by such methods. Feigl has clear affinity with Dewey's opposition to ultimate values in Chapter 2, section 2, as well as with his social morality, and his faith in reason and in processes of scientific inquiry.

The disposition Feigl favors as an educational end-in-view is a complex commitment to scientific method and social welfare, with an interest in humanity which never transcends the natural world and a view of rationality which never divorces scientific method from moral concern. Indeed, Feigl's rationality shows itself to be clearly dispositional in a moral sense in his references to such inclinations as "adherence to principles of justice, equity, or impartiality," and "the abstention from coercion and violence in the settlement of conflicts of interest." Other aspects of rationality are dispositional by implication. Education is to foster these "virtues of thought" by developing respect for skills of accurate communication, logical reasoning and objectivity, and the determination to use them.

Feigl's emphasis on rationality and science is the bridge to the viewpoints of this section. Like Feigl, both Peters and Dewey differ radically in outlook from Buber and Plato. The search for eternal values is gone. The Platonic elevation of reason for its supposed power of breaking out of the natural world to perceive a reality beyond it is re-

[4] *Ibid.*, p. 210.

placed by reason valued solely for its power of perceiving the natural world and the experience occurring in it.

Reliance on reason and experience is common to Peters and Dewey, but the emphasis is differently placed by the two. Peters' contribution is an illustration of analytical inquiry within the empirical world. Dewey's main concern is with experience itself and with ways of improving its quality. Peters is predominantly analytical, Dewey predominantly normative.

As an analyst, Peters sees his task to be primarily that of clarifying the language of moral education so that the problems of this area can be brought into sharper focus. Before educators speak of developing dispositions of character, they should ask what "character" and "trait" mean, Peters explains, and how one's "character" is different from one's "nature." Then they will realize that there are three ways of speaking of character: (1) in a non-committal way, referring to the selection of rules a person has assimilated in regulating his conduct; (2) in a way that refers to a distinctive pattern or style of traits when one speaks of a person as having a certain type of character; and (3) in a way that extols, as when saying that a person *has* character, referring possibly to qualities such as "integrity, incorruptibility, or consistency." More specifically, the educator should be clear, if he is to influence a child toward moral behavior, on which rules a growing child should absorb, and what *type* of character or pattern of traits is to be fostered. He should ask how rules are to be learned (as habits, or with insight and understanding), and, if the purpose is to assist the child's development toward the stage when he can be said to *have* character, how he can be educated toward self-control and self-regulation of conduct. How far Peters has moved from Plato, for whom moral education of children meant dispositions that rubbed off as habits on impressionable minds!

The dispositions Peters favors become apparent before he states them: "an autonomous type of character who follows rules in a rational discriminating manner, and who also has character." For Peters, the higher order principles (for intelligent application and revision of rules) are impartiality and the consideration of interests. What Plato reserved for the training of his ruling class, Peters makes available for all. His ideal is clearly that of a rational man and the dispositions he favors are strongly intellectual.

Dewey also begins by analyzing character, but his analysis is not of word meanings. Dewey attempts to show that character is *psychologically* a "capacity of social functioning." Whereas Peters stresses reason, Dewey points to the importance of habits in character formation, habits that will lead reliably to action. Dewey favors the type of character reflected in traits of initiative, insistence, persistence, courage, and industry. The man who *has* character, he argues, is one marked by capacity for forceful, decisive action in the social interest. Although habit formation is prominent in Dewey's thoughts on moral dispositions, intellect and emotion also play a part. Intellect imparts judgment as a sense of proportion, and gives the ability to comprehend the main elements in a situation. Emotion is needed for its sensitiveness to others' interests.

In the second selection from Dewey, the normative impulse is more conspicuous. Again habit is emphasized in its power of modifying dispositions, but the dispositions are related more positively to improvement of social living. Dispositions such as honesty have no virtue in isolation; they acquire significance only in relation to many other dispositions in the fabric of effective social activity. The moral and the social, for Dewey, are identical, and the "essence of morals" is the disposition to maintain the capacity for balancing what one gives and receives in social relationships. To return to his ideal of democracy, Dewey favors most highly a dedication to social welfare, a commitment that can be effective only if assimilated completely within the individual's own value system. In this stress on personal orientation, Dewey anticipates the educational ends-in-view of Part III.

Dispositions Associated with Absolutes

Martin Buber: The Education of Character[1]

Education worthy of the name is essentially education of character. For the genuine educator does not merely consider individual functions of his pupil, as one intending to teach him only to know or to be capable of certain definite things; but his concern is always the person as a whole, both in the actuality in which he lives before you now and in his possibilities, what he can become. But in this way, as a whole in reality and potentiality, a man can be conceived either as personality, that is, as a unique spiritual-physical form with all the forces dormant in it, or as character, that is, as the link between what this individual is and the sequence of his actions and attitudes. Between these two modes of conceiving the pupil in his wholeness there is a fundamental difference. Personality is something which in its growth remains essentially outside the influence of the educator; but to assist in the moulding of character is his greatest task. Personality is a completion, only character is a task. One may cultivate and enhance personality, but in education one can and one must aim at character.

* * * *

... In order to penetrate to the real difficulties in the education of character we have to examine critically the concept of character itself.

Kerschensteiner in his well-known essay on *The Concept and Education of Character* distinguished between "character in the most general sense," by which he means "a man's attitude to his human surroundings, which is constant and is expressed in his actions," and real "ethical character," which he defines as "a special attitude, and one which in action gives the preference before all others to absolute values." If we begin by accepting this distinction unreservedly—and undeniably there is some truth in it—we are faced with such heavy odds in all education of character in our time that the very possibility of it seems doubtful.

The "absolute values" which Kerschensteiner refers to cannot, of course, be meant to have only subjective validity for the person concerned. Don Juan finds absolute and subjective value in seducing the

[1] From Martin Buber, *Between Man and Man*, translated and with an introduction by R.G. Smith. London: William Collins, Sons and Co., Fontana Library, 1961, pp. 132, 136-137, 139-140, 142-147, with omissions. Reprinted by permission of Routledge & Kegan-Paul Ltd., and The Macmillan Company.

greatest possible number of women, and the dictator sees it in the greatest possible accumulation of power. "Absolute validity" can only relate to universal values and norms, the existence of which the person concerned recognizes and acknowledges. But to deny the presence of universal values and norms of absolute validity—that is the conspicuous tendency of our age. This tendency is not, as is sometimes supposed, directed merely against the sanctioning of the norms by religion, but against their universal character and absolute validity, against their claim to be of a higher order than man and to govern the whole of mankind. In our age values and norms are not permitted to be anything but expressions of the life of a group which translates its own needs into the language of objective claims, until at last the group itself, for example a nation, is raised to an absolute value—and moreover to the only value. Then this splitting up into groups so pervades the whole of life that it is no longer possible to re-establish a sphere of values common to mankind, and a commandment to mankind is no longer observed. As this tendency grows the basis for the development of what Kerschensteiner means by moral character steadily diminishes. How, under these circumstances, can the task of educating character be completed?

*   *   *   *

. . . In order to enter into a personal relation with the absolute, it is first necessary to be a person again, to rescue one's real personal self from the fiery jaws of collectivism which devours all selfhood. The desire to do this is latent in the pain the individual suffers through his distorted relation to his own self. Again and again he dulls the pain with a subtle poison and thus suppresses the desire as well. To keep the pain awake, to waken the desire—that is the first task of everyone who regrets the obscuring of eternity. It is also the first task of the genuine educator in our time.

The man for whom absolute values in a universal sense do not exist cannot be made to adopt "an attitude which in action gives the preference over all others to absolute values." But what one can inculcate in him is the desire to attain once more to a real attitude, and that is, the desire to become a person following the only way that leads to this goal to-day.

*   *   *   *

The great character can be conceived neither as a system of maxims nor as a system of habits. It is peculiar to him to act from the whole of his substance. That is, it is peculiar to him to react in accordance with the uniqueness of every situation which challenges him as an active person. Of course there are all sorts of similarities in different situations; one can construct types of situations, one can always find to what section the particular situation belongs, and draw what is appropriate from the hoard of established maxims and habits, apply the appropriate maxim, bring into operation the appropriate habit. But what is untypical in the particular situation remains unnoticed and unanswered. To me that seems the same as if, having ascertained the sex of a new-born child, one were immediately to establish its type as well, and put all the children of one type into a common cradle on which not the individual name but the name of the type was inscribed. In spite of all similarities every living situation has, like a new-born child, a new face, that has never been before and will never come again. It demands of you a reaction which cannot be prepared beforehand. It demands nothing of what is past. It demands presence, responsibility; it demands you. I call a great character one who by his actions and attitudes satisfies the claim of situations out of deep readiness to respond with his whole life, and in such a way that the sum of his actions and attitudes expresses at the same time the unity of his being in its willingness to accept responsibility. As his being is unity, the unity of accepted responsibility, his active life, too, coheres into unity. And one might perhaps say that for him there rises a unity out of the situations he has responded to in responsibility, the indefinable unity of a moral destiny.

All this does not mean that the great character is beyond the acceptance of norms. No responsible person remains a stranger to norms. But the command inherent in a genuine norm never becomes a maxim and the fulfilment of it never a habit. Any command that a great character takes to himself in the course of his development does not act in him as part of his consciousness or as material for building up his exercises, but remains latent in a basic layer of his substance until it reveals itself to him in a concrete way. What it has to tell him is revealed whenever a situation arises which demands of him a solution of which till then he had perhaps no idea. Even the most universal norm will at times be recognized only in a very special situation.

*   *   *   *

Of course, it may be asked whether the educator should really start "from above," whether, in fixing his goal,[1] the hope of finding a great character, who is bound to be the exception, should be his starting-point; for in his methods of educating character he will always have to

---

[1] At this stage, in the mind of the educator, "objective" would be the appropriate term according to the terminology adopted in this book (Editors note).

take into consideration the others, the many. To this I reply that the educator would not have the right to do so if a method inapplicable to these others were to result. In fact, however, his very insight into the structure of a great character helps him to find the way by which alone (as I have indicated) he can begin to influence also the victims of the collective Moloch, pointing out to them the sphere in which they themselves suffer—namely, their relation to their own selves. From this sphere he must elicit the values which he can make credible and desirable to his pupils. That is what insight into the structure of a great character helps him to do.

A section of the young is beginning to feel to-day that because of their absorption by the collective, something important and irreplaceable is lost to them—personal responsibility for life and the world. These young people, it is true, do not realize that their blind devotion to the collective, e.g. to a party, was not a genuine act of their personal life, they do not realize that it sprang, rather, from the fear of being left, in this age of confusion, to rely on themselves, on a self which no longer receives its direction from eternal values. Thus they do not yet realize that their devotion was fed on the unconscious desire to have responsibility removed from them by an authority in which they believe or want to believe. They do not yet realize that this devotion was an escape. I repeat, the young people I am speaking of do not yet realize this. But they are beginning to notice that he who no longer, with his whole being, decides what he does or does not, and assumes responsibility for it, becomes sterile in soul. And a sterile soul ceases to be a soul.

This is where the educator can begin and should begin. He can help the feeling that something is lacking to grow into the clarity of consciousness and into the force of desire. He can awaken in young people the courage to shoulder life again. He can bring before his pupils the image of a great character who denies no answer to life and the world, but accepts responsibility for everything essential that he meets. He can show his pupils this image without the fear that those among them who most of all need discipline and order will drift into a craving for aimless freedom: on the contrary, he can teach them in this way to recognize that discipline and order too are starting-points on the way towards self-responsibility. He can show that even the great character is not born perfect, that the unity of his being has first to mature before expressing itself in the sequence of his actions and attitudes. But unity itself, unity of the person, unity of the lived life, has to be emphasized again and again
    ... It is the longing for personal unity, from which must be born a unity of mankind, which the educator should lay hold of and strengthen

in his pupils. Faith in this unity and the will to achieve it is not a "return" to individualism, but a step beyond all the dividedness of individualism and collectivism. A great and full relation between man and man can only exist between unified and responsible persons. That is why it is much more rarely found in the totalitarian collective than in any historically earlier form of society; much more rarely also in the authoritarian party than in any earlier form of free association. Genuine education of character is genuine education for community.

In a generation which has had this kind of upbringing the desire will also be kindled to behold again the eternal values, to hear again the language of the eternal norm. He who knows inner unity, the innermost life of which is mystery, learns to honour the mystery in all its forms. The educator who helps to bring man back to his own unity will help to put him again face to face with God.

Plato: A Higher Reality[1]

(Socrates is speaking with Glaucon)

'This, then, which imparts truth to the things that are known and the power of knowing to the knower, you may affirm to be the Form of the good. It is the cause of knowledge and truth, and you may conceive it as being known, but while knowledge and truth are both beautiful, you will be right in thinking it other and fairer than these. And as in the other world it is right to think light and sight sunlike, but not right to think them the sun, so here it is right to think both knowledge and truth like the good, but not right to think either of them the good. The state or nature of the good must be honoured still more highly.'

'You speak of an incalculable beauty,' he said, 'if it gives knowledge and truth, and itself excels them in beauty. Surely you do not mean that this is pleasure?'

'Do not blaspheme,' I said. 'Rather consider its image in this further aspect.'

'How?'

'I fancy that you will say that the sun gives to visible objects not only the power of being seen, but also their generation and growth and nourishment, not being itself generation.'

'Of course not.'

'Then you may say of the objects of knowledge that not only their being known comes from the good, but their existence and being also

[1] From Plato, *The Republic*, translated by Dr. A. D. Lindsay. Everyman's Library Edition. London: J. M. Dent & Sons, 1935, Book VI, pp. 203, 210-212, with omissions. Reprinted by permission of E. P. Dutton & Co., Inc.

come from it, though the good is not itself being but transcends even being in dignity and power?'

'If you will set the upward ascent and the seeing of the things in the upper world with the upward journey of the soul to the intelligible sphere, you will have my surmise; and that is what you are anxious to have. Whether it be actually true, God knows. But this is how it appears to me. In the world of knowledge the Form of the good is perceived last and with difficulty, but when it is seen it must be inferred that it is the cause of all that is right and beautiful in all things, producing in the visible world light and the lord of light, and being itself lord in the intelligible world and the giver of truth and reason, and this Form of the good must be seen by whosoever would act wisely in public or in private.'

'I agree with you,' he said, 'so far as I am capable.'

'Come, then,' I said, 'and agree with me in this also; and don't be surprised that they who have come thus far are unwilling to trouble themselves with mortal affairs, and that their souls are ever eager to dwell above. For this is but natural if the image we have related is true.'

'It is,' he said.

'Then do you think it at all surprising,' I said, 'if one who has come from divine visions to human miseries plays a sorry part and appears very ridiculous when, with eyes still confused and before he has got properly used to the darkness that is round him, he is compelled to contend in law courts or elsewhere concerning the shadows of the just or the images which throw those shadows, or to dispute concerning the manner in which those images are conceived by men who have never seen real justice?'

*   *   *   *

'Education, then,' I said, 'will be an art of doing this, an art of conversion, and will consider in what manner the soul will be turned round most easily and effectively. Its aim will not be to implant vision in the instrument of sight. It will regard it as already possessing that, but as being turned in a wrong direction, and not looking where it ought, and it will try to set this right.'

'That seems probable,' he said.

'Now most of the virtues which are commonly said to belong to the soul seem to resemble the bodily virtues. They seem to be really implanted by habit and exercise where they have not previously existed. But the virtue of wisdom evidently does in reality belong to something much more divine, which never loses its power, but which from conversion becomes useful and advantageous, or again useless and harmful.'

Plato: The Forming of Dispositions[1]

(Socrates speaks with Adeimantus)

'Then shall we carelessly and without more ado allow our children to hear any casual stories told by any casual persons, and so to receive into their souls views of life for the most part at variance with those which we think they ought to hold when they come to man's estate?'

'No, we shall certainly not allow that.'

'Our first duty then, it seems, is to set a watch over the makers of stories, to select every beautiful story they make, and reject any that are not beautiful. Then we shall persuade nurses and mothers to tell those selected stories to the children. Thus will they shape their souls with stories far more than they can shape their bodies with their hands. But we shall have to throw away most of the stories they tell now.'

*   *   *   *

'And we shall strictly forbid,' I said, 'all stories of gods making war on or plotting against or fighting other gods. To begin with, they are not true; and besides, those who are to guard our city must think it the most deadly sin to quarrel easily with one another. The fights of the giants and the other many and varied strifes of gods and heroes with kinsfolk and friends must not be told them in story or woven on their tapestry. But if we can in any way find stories to persuade them that no citizen has ever hated another, and that such a thing is impious, it is these rather that our old men and women must tell to the young children, and when they grow older, the poets must be compelled to make stories for them of a like nature. But the binding of Hera by her son, or the hurling of Hephaestus from heaven by his father, when his mother was being beaten and he tried to defend her, and all the tales of the battles of the giants that Homer has made, these stories we shall not receive into our city, whether their purport be allegorical or not. For the child is unable to discriminate between what is allegory and what is not; whatever he receives and believes at that early age is apt to become permanent and indelible. For these reasons, perhaps, we must do everything in our power to contrive that the first stories our children are told shall teach virtue in the fairest way.'

[1] From Plato, *The Republic*, translated by Dr. A. D. Lindsay. Everyman's Library Edition. London: J. M. Dent & Sons, 1935, Book III, pp. 58-59, 77-78, 84-85, 95, with omissions. Reprinted by permission of E. P. Dutton & Co., Inc.

'Then if we are to be faithful to our original position, that our guardians must be released from all other handicrafts to be in all earnestness craftsmen of the freedom of the city, and must do nothing that does not contribute to this end, then they must neither do nor imitate anything else. And if they imitate, they must imitate from childhood subjects befitting their vocation, brave, temperate, pious, free men, and the like; but meanness and any other ugly thing they must neither do nor be able to imitate, lest from the imitation they become infected with the reality. Have you not noticed that the practice of imitation, if it is begun in youth and persisted in, leaves its impress upon character and nature, on body and voice and mind?'

'Yes, certainly,' he said.

*   *   *   *

'The man of measured character in the first place, when he came in his narration to the speech or action of a good man, would, I think, wish to speak in the good man's person, and would not be ashamed of that kind of imitation. He would imitate the good man with especial thoroughness in his cautious and wise actions, less carefully and to a less degree when he was overcome by disease, or love, or by drunkenness, or any other misfortune. But when he comes to someone unworthy of him, he will not be willing to liken himself seriously to his inferior. He may for a little when he is doing a good action, but apart from that he will be ashamed, partly because he is not in the way of imitating such people, but also from a repugnance to moulding and conforming himself to the morals of inferior men whom he deliberately despises; unless it be for mere amusement.'

(Socrates speaks with Glaucon)

'Then we must speak to our poets and compel them to impress upon their poems only the image of the good, or not to make poetry in our city. And we must speak to the other craftsmen and forbid them to leave the impress of that which is evil in character, unrestrained, mean and ugly, on their likenesses of living creatures, or their houses, or on anything else which they make. He that cannot obey must not be allowed to ply his trade in our city. For we would not have our guardians reared among images of evil as in a foul pasture, and there day by day and little by little gather many impressions from all that surrounds them, taking them all in until at last a great mass of evil gathers in their inmost souls, and they know it not. No, we must seek out those craftsmen who have the happy gift of tracing out the nature of the fair and graceful, that our young men may dwell as in a health-giving region where all that surrounds them is beneficent, whencesoever from fair works of art there smite upon their eyes and ears an affluence like a wind bringing health from happy regions, which, though they know it not, leads them from their earliest years into likeness and friendship and harmony with the principle of beauty.'

' A nobler manner of education,' he said, 'there could not be.'

'Then, Glaucon,' I said, 'is not musical education of paramount importance for those reasons, because rhythm and harmony enter most powerfully into the innermost part of the soul and lay forcible hands upon it, bearing grace with them, so making graceful him who is rightly trained, and him who is not, the reverse? Is it not a further reason that he who has been rightly trained in music would be quick to observe all works of art that were defective or ugly, and all natural objects that failed in beauty? They would displease him, and rightly; but beautiful things he would praise, and receiving them with joy into his soul, would be nourished by them and become noble and good. Ugly things he would rightly condemn, and hate even in his youth before he was capable of reason; but when reason comes he would welcome her as one he knows, with whom his training has made him familiar.'

'It is more likely,' I said, 'that both music and gymnastics are meant especially for the soul.'

'How?'

'Have you never noticed,' I said, 'how a lifelong training in gymnastics without music affects the character, or what is the effect of the opposite training?'

'To what do you refer?' he said.

'To fierceness and hardness on the one hand,' I said, 'and softness and gentleness on the other.'

'I know,' he said, 'exclusive devotion to gymnastics turns men out fiercer than need be, while the same devotion to music makes them softer than is good for them.'

'Yes,' I said, 'it is the spirited element in their nature that produces the fierceness; well trained it would be bravery, but if it is strained over much it will turn into hardness and surliness, and naturally enough.'

'I agree with you,' he said.

'Then is not gentleness involved in the philosophic nature; but if it relaxes too much into gentleness, the temperament will be made too soft, while the right training will make it both gentle and orderly, will it not?'

'It will.'

'Now we assert that our guardians must have both those elements of character?'

'They must.'

'Then must not these be made to accord with one another?'

'Surely.'

'And when this accordance has been reached, is not the soul both temperate and brave?'

'Certainly.'

'But when there is discord, is not the soul cowardly and boorish?'

'Yes.'

H. Feigl: Ends and Means of Education[1]

The scientific outlook in philosophy proposed by the logical empiricists has no room for "absolute values"—if this phrase is understood to mean values that could be demonstrated or otherwise justified independently of any reference to human needs, interests, and ideals as they naturally arise in the bio-psycho-socioeconomic-historical matrix of civilization. Our age of scientific enlightenment requires a new form of emotional and moral maturity: We shall have to learn to *live* with our knowledge about ourselves: to combine scientific, penetrating insight with serious moral and social commitments; to acquire the ability to use our knowledge wisely and humanely. There are many who find no difficulty in this. But there are others who do not feel secure except within the frame of dogmatic creeds. And there are still others who, having lost their religious or their social-political absolute faiths, feel completely at sea and resort to a "philosophy" of nausea, despair, and spasmodic irrational action. Such a philosophy is exemplified in some of the German and French forms of existentialism. It is not fully clear at present to what extent the inherited constitution and the life-experiences of an individual are responsible for these attitudes or character traits, or for dispositions inclining them in these directions. Fuller insight into the factors that determine a person's outlook upon life will ultimately help in the elimination of infantile fixations and in the prevention of regressions to less mature levels of development.

The scientific humanist does not engage in the search for absolutes, the quest for the indubitable; but he is nevertheless able firmly to hold to the truths which experience has sufficiently substantiated and to the attitudes which experience has sufficiently endorsed. He is not disturbed by the impossibility of demonstrating that his beliefs and attitudes are

[1] From H. Feigl, "Aims of Education for Our Age of Science," *The Fifty-fourth Yearbook of the National Society for the Study of Education, Part 1.* Chicago: University of Chicago Press, 1955, pp. 331-333, 335-336, 338, with omissions. Reprinted by permission of the National Society for the Study of Education.

necessarily the only ones that are "absolutely valid." The scientific humanist thinks and acts within a frame of standards and criteria which he feels has sufficient *practical* justification not to be called into question on every occasion of doubt. He attempts to resolve doubts first *within* this frame, but he is entirely willing to reconsider the frame itself and, if necessary, to replace it by a new one. Psychological studies have made it fairly clear that the tolerance of uncertainty, of doubt, of dilemmatic quandries is more marked in what also, on other grounds, would be recognized as the more "grown-up," the maturer kind of personality. Emotional immaturity often expresses itself in a dogmatic attitude.

The scientific humanist refuses to anchor his beliefs and valuations in the unknown or the unknowable. He recognizes the illusions engendered by wishful thinking that underlie the other-worldly (transcendent) beliefs of those who cling to the orthodoxies of theology or metaphysics. He repudiates as worthless sophistry the medieval and latter-day theological or metaphysical "demonstrations." Logical analysis shows clearly the reckless and irresponsible extensions of the usage of ordinary language when applied to the "absolutes" of transcendent speculation. The humanist also suspects that the much-vaunted "humility" of those who submit to an absolute authority (be it religious or political), in some cases, amounts to a camouflaged conceit or arrogance. The claims of "higher" knowledge or of special power or privilege are only too transparently self-aggrandizing delusions. Equally obvious in a psychological way are the techniques of promising rewards or threatening with punishment in the hereafter. The humanist can look only with contempt at such bribery or blackmail. Mankind would be in a deplorable position if it depended on such crude devises for the enforcement of its moral principles.

In our age of scientific enlightenment, human knowledge and human love and sympathy are the only firm foundations on which moral conduct can be built. The message of brotherly love combined with the message of justice, the ethical core of many of the world's religions (but without the theological superstructure), is, of course, wholeheartedly accepted by present-day naturalistic humanists. It is an elementary fact, fully substantiated by modern psychology, that the constructive tendencies of love and sympathy are apt to be inhibited or to be turned into aggression, cruelty, and violence through frustration or deprivation. Whatever original, aggressive impulses there are in the behavior of the normal child can be sublimated and thus guided into channels of socially constructive action by proper educational guidance. It is a common human experience that our actions are apt to be socially most valuable if they spring from deeply benevolent impulses. It is equally clear that we achieve peace of mind under these same conditions.

*   *   *   *

. . . The classical Aristotelean conception of man as the rational animal—all too frequent manifestations of irrationality to the contrary notwithstanding—may still be a good beginning. But it is indispensable to explicate fully and precisely what this "rationality" to be fostered in education signifies in sum and substance.

"Rationality" connotes a variety of virtues of thought and conduct. The following list may not be complete, but it will be sufficiently suggestive:

1. *Clarity of Thought.*   This implies the meaningful use of language, the ability to distinguish sense from nonsense and thus avoid gratuitous perplexities over unanswerable questions. It also implies a sufficient degree of specification of definition of meanings so that communication may be as unambiguous and concepts be as precise as the task on hand requires.

2. *Consistency and Conclusiveness of Reasoning.*   This is "logicality" in the narrower sense of absence of self-contradictions and of analytically necessary implications between the premises and the conclusions of valid deductive arguments. Conformity with the principles of formal logic insures fulfilment of this requirement.

3. *Factual Adequacy and Reliability of Knowledge Claims.*   These are the virtues of thought usually summarized under the caption "truth." Truth may be semantically defined as correspondence of statements and facts. But this rather formal definition is insufficient if a characterization of the confirmation of truth is to be given. Wherever a complete confrontation of statement and corresponding fact is impossible, principles of inductive probability for the partial and/or indirect verification of generalizations, hypotheses, or theories have to be respected. Generally the degree of confirmation (or of the reliability) of factual statements is to be maximized in accordance with the rules of inductive logic. Wherever the evidence is too weak, belief should be withheld until further evidence turns up to decide the issue on hand.

4. *Objectivity of Knowledge Claims.*   This comprises intersubjectivity and impartiality in cognitive issues. Objectivity in this sense involves not only absence of personal or cultural bias but also the requirement that knowledge claims be testable by any person sufficiently equipped with intelligence and the instrumental devices for performing the test of the knowledge-claim in question.

5. Rationality of Purposive Behavior. Rationality in this sense may be explicated as the main feature of behavior which achieves its purposes by a proper choice of means. Behavior which defeats its own purposes is generally considered "irrational." This criterion of rationality is closely related to a similar but more specialized concept in economics. Generally speaking, we have here a conception of rationality which amounts to a minimum-maximum ("minimax") principle according to which a maximum of positive value is to be produced by means which involve a minimum of negative value.

6. Moral Rationality. This comprises: *(a)* Adherence to principles of justice, equity, or impartiality. If there is no morally relevant or sufficient reason to allow greater privileges to one person than another, they are to be *equal* before the moral law. This exclusion of special privilege rules out the sort of arbitrary arrogation of rights on the part of individuals who are unwilling to accept the correlative obligations. *(b)* The abstention from coercion and violence in the settlement of conflicts of interest. "Appeal to reason" in the sense of all the connotations of "rationality" thus far enumerated (from *1* through *6a*) is deemed as the only morally acceptable method for the adjudication of disputes.

*　　*　　*　　*

Science, by way of a reductive fallacy, is still regarded as essentially materialistic, and thus as incapable of accounting for the "higher things of life." And these "higher things" are still regarded as essentially beyond the reach of scientific inquiry because of theological or metaphysical preconceptions which, owing to cultural lag, still survive in much of the thinking and even the language of our day. From the point of view of a scientific humanism, the aesthetic values, the values of the moral life and the values of love and friendship, are not in the least endangered by any explanation of their origins or functions that psychology and the social sciences may contribute. Only those who insist that the higher values of life are sustained by supernatural powers will find the scientific outlook severely sobering or disappointing. But once the other-worldly and obscurantist conceit is abandoned, our lives will be enriched by a better understanding of ourselves.

Rational and Empirical Dispositions

R. S. Peters: Moral Education and the Psychology of Character[1]

Character and character-traits

It is no accident that the concept of 'character' is appropriately used in contexts of individual adaptation; for etymologically the word 'character', like the word 'trait', which is often associated with it, is connected with making a distinguishing mark. 'Character' comes from the field of engraving; hence we talk naturally of the delineation of character. 'Trait' comes from the cognate field of drawing. In their figurative sense, when applied to human beings, they are both used to bring out what is *distinctive* about people.

It seems to me, too, that there is another important similarity between the term 'character' and the term 'trait' which often leads to hyphenation. Their significance is primarily adverbial. They usually indicate a *manner* or *style* of behaving without any definite implication of directedness or aversion—unlike the terms 'motive', 'attitude', and 'sentiment'. 'Trait', however, covers countless manners of behaving. Allport claims that 18,000 words in the English language are trait names.[2] Traits of character are obviously a selection from these—for example traits like selfishness, honesty, puctuality, considerateness, and meanness. Such terms, like all trait terms, are primarily adverbial in significance. They do not, like greed or sexual desire, indicate the sort of goals that a man tends to pursue, but the manner in which he pursues them. A man who is ruthless, selfish, honest, punctual, considerate, does not necessarily have any particular goals; rather he behaves in a certain manner, according to or not according to certain rules. And, I suppose, the connection with regulation is fundamental for bringing out what distinguishes character-traits from other sorts of traits—for instance those which we describe as a matter of temperament. Character-traits are shown in the sort of things a man can *decide* to be, where it may be a matter of forcing himself to do something in the face of social pressures or persistent temptations. In this way a man's character is contrasted with his nature. A man just is stupid or lacking in vitality; he cannot decide to be either of these. But he can decide to be more or less honest or selfish.[3] His

---

[1] From R. S. Peters, "The Psychology of Character," *Philosophy*, Macmillan (Journals), London, vol. XXXVII, no. 139, 1962, pp. 38-47. Reprinted by permission of the Royal Institute of Philosophy.

[2] Allport, G. W. *Personality* (Henry Holt, New York, 1937), p. 303.

inclinations and desires, which are part of his 'nature', may suggest goals; but such inclinations and desires only enter into what we call a man's 'character' in so far as he chooses to satisfy them in a certain manner, in accordance with rules of efficiency like persistently, carefully, doggedly, painstakingly, or in accordance with rules of social appropriateness like honestly, fairly, considerately, and ruthlessly. Greed is not a character-trait if it means just an appetite for money or food; but it becomes a character-trait as soon as it carries the suggestion that this appetite is exercised ruthlessly or selfishly at someone else's expense, in other words in a certain manner. A craving for a beef-steak, a lust for a pretty girl reveal a man's nature, not his character. His character is revealed in what he does about them, in the manner in which he regulates, or fails to regulate them.

The point is often made that talk of character occurs in contexts of praise and blame. Indeed psychologists since McDougall have perhaps shied off character because of it. To quote Allport: 'Character enters the situation only when this personal effort is judged from the standpoint of some code'.[4] But my guess is that the fundamental connection is between character and some sort of personal effort. The judgment from the point of view of a code comes in because it is largely for his efforts and decisions that a man is praised or blamed rather than for his desires and inclinations. Nowell-Smith, too, stresses the connection between character and praise and blame when he says 'Pleasure and pain, reward and punishment, are the rudders by means of which moral character is moulded; and "moral character" is just that set of dispositions that can be moulded by these means'.[5] Stupidity and vitality cannot be moulded by this sort of regulation; so we usually do not regard them as traits of character. But this is surely a mistake; for Nowell-Smith's statement that moral 'character *is just* that set of dispositions that can be moulded by these means' suggests that the connection is a necessary one. But we can surely be completely hazy about the spheres in which praise and blame, reward and punishment are in fact effective; and yet we can talk quite confidently about a person's character. Also there are many 'dispositions' which can be altered by praise and blame that might not be regarded as part of a man's 'character'—e.g. his wants and wishes. There may well be, of course, a close connection between what a person can decide to do or force himself to do by personal effort and what he

[3] I am indebted to Mrs. Foot for this point which she stressed when replying to an early version of this paper which I read to the Oxford Philosophical Society in March 1958.

[4] G. W. Allport, *op. cit.*, p. 51.

[5] P. H. Nowell-Smith, *Ethics* (Penguin, Harmondsworth, 1954), p. 304.

can be made to do by praise and blame or by reward and punishment. But the connection is a contingent one. And there may indeed be, via the notion of decision, a necessary connection between a person's character and those dispositions which can *in principle* be moulded by praise and blame; for moulding by praise and blame presupposes the decision of the moulded, in a way which something like brain surgery does not.

There is surely the point, too, that if any term is to be linked with social assessment Allport's favoured term 'personality' is an obvious candidate. Allport, of course, uses the term as an omnibus technical term to cover more or less everything that a man is; but such a generalized usage leaves rather high and dry the perfectly good use of the term in ordinary language which, like the term 'character', picks out certain distinctive features of a man. For a man's personality is very much the mask or appearance which he presents to others; a man 'with personality' or 'with a strong personality' is a man whose behaviour is assessed as impinging in certain ways on others. It has not the same suggestion of inner effort and decision as has 'character'. A man's personality flowers or develops; it is not built up by his decisions as is his character. The criteria of assessment are, of course, very different. But certainly to say of man that he has 'personality' is to praise him as much as to say that he has 'character'. But it is to praise him according to different criteria. What Allport means, surely, is that character is connected inseparably with the following of rules. But as one of the most important things to say about man is that he is a rule-following animal, the concept of 'character' should be one of the most indispensable terms in psychology.

This brief excursion into the comparison between the terms 'character' and 'personality' has shown that it is difficult enough to decide what in general we mean when we speak of a person's character as distinct from his nature, his temperament, and his personality; but the matter is further complicated by the fact that there seem to be at least three ways in which we can talk of 'character'. We can speak (a) in a non-committal way of a man's character, we can speak of him (b) as having a type of character, and we can speak of him (c) as having character. These distinctions, so it seems to me, are important for discussing matters concerned with the psychology of character, so it will be necessary to elucidate them in more detail.

Three Ways of Speaking of 'Character'

(a) The non-committal use.   I suppose the most common use of 'character' is when we use the term as a way of referring to the sum-total of a man's character-traits. An individual is brought up in an elaborate

system of codes and conventions. To speak of his character is to speak of the particular selection of rules which he has, as it were, absorbed in regulating his conduct both in relation to others and in pursuit of his more personal ends. If a servant is given a character—or was—her future employer is informed of the particular traits which she tends to exhibit, the part of the code which is, as it were, stamped upon her. And it was presumably with 'character' in this sense that the abortive Hartshorne and May enquiry was concerned.

(b) Types of character.   In the second way of speaking of 'character', some distinctive pattern of traits is indicated or some distinctive style in which the traits are exhibited. We speak of the anal character, for instance. Presumably this second way of speaking of a type of character is connected with characters in a play. Characters, in this sense, are depicted or delineated either with some dominant trait emphasized or with a typical exaggeration or distortion of a range of traits. Parsimony, for instance, not only is an exaggeration of the 'normal' trait of being careful with money; but in characters like L'Avare it becomes generalized over a whole range of behaviour. This is the sense of 'character' beloved of characterologists.[6] Usually a style of life is sketched which is related to some central trait. Alternatively a whole range of traits is exhibited in a consistently distorted or exaggerated manner. Some of Hardy's characters illustrate this other way in which one can have a type of character; they have a peculiarly obsessive style of following rules like men who are excessively punctual, polite, and precise. Freud's theory of character-

---

[6] Having a type of character should, I think, be distinguished from 'being a character', although it might be said that, under certain conditions, a man who has a certain type of character could be called *a* character. For the point about 'being a character' is that the phrase is used in contexts where we wish to stress some distinctive style of conduct which is *amusing*. A character is, as it were, an original; but he must display oddities which are droll or amusing. Hitler or the Marquis de Sade had types of character; but it would be very strange to refer to them as characters. For we only speak of people being characters when they display idiosyncrasies which, though systematic, are morally indifferent. A degree of indulgence is, as it were, extended to their eccentricities by calling them 'characters'. If we referred to the penurious man, who has a type of character, as a character, this would be a bit unusual; but it would be possible. For we would be stressing the entertainment value of his style of life. But we could not conceivably look at Hitler or the Marquis de Sade in this indulgent manner. We would never, therefore, speak of them as characters. So some types of character may be possessed by people who are also characters; but the concepts are not co-extensive. (I am largely indebted to A. P. Griffiths for these points and for his comments on the whole paper.

traits is largely an attempt to trace the genesis of character in this second sense.[7] However, not all 'types of character' present such a depressing picture. There is the 'genital character' of the Freudian school, whose behaviour shows consistency but of a different order. For he regulates his following of rules in accordance with principles of a higher order like those of prudence or respect for persons, and varies them intelligently, making distinctions and exceptions to match relevant differences in the situations in which he is acting. In the case of the penurious man, by contrast, there is no such intelligent adaptation. Similarly the other anal type of character, who has a characteristic exaggeration or distortion of a range of traits, behaves in a way which is irrelevant to changes in situations. The norm-ridden man, like the pedant or over-scrupulous man, always goes further in regulation than the situation warrants. There is, too, the further point that argument and persuasion seem to make little difference to the style in question. And if the rule-following is backed by justifications, they can usually be regarded only as rationalisations. For no counter arguments or fresh evidence will bring about any change.

The distinctiveness and consistency of the rule-following of the autonomous or 'genital' type of character, on the other hand, is of quite a difficult sort. Such a man will not necessarily be careful with money on all occasions. Indeed he may well present an *appearance* of inconsistency to the observer. He may be frugal in entertaining his friends but more lavish in entertaining his family; he may not insist on tidiness at home but may insist on it in his office. But these variations in rule-following cannot be correlated either with the strength of his inclinations or with the strength of social pressures. He follows rules for which he sees some point and he modifies them to take account of relevant differences in situations; and the point to a large extent, is determined by his adherence to higher order principles, e.g. that of the consideration of interests. And we usually have to see his behaviour from the inside, from his point of view, before we understand it. Roback, in his classic on *The Psychology of Character,* defines 'character' as 'An enduring psychodisposition to inhibit instinctive impulses in accordance with a physical regulative principle . . . the man of character in the full sense of the word exercises a distributed inhibitory power in keeping with a general principle which subsumes under its authority more negative a specialised maxims'.[8] 'Inhibition', here, perhaps conveys too suggestion. For

[7] See R. S. Peters, *Freud's Theory of Moral Development in Relation to that of Piaget.* Brit. Journ. Ed. Psych. Vol. XXX, Part III, Nov. 1960.

[8] A. Roback, *The Psychology of Character* (Kegan Paul, London, 1928), p. 452.

'character' can be shown in encouraging and shaping natural tendencies; it need not always be revealed in their inhibition.[9]

(c) Having character. We come now to the third way of speaking of 'character' which is clearly different from having a type of character. For Kant had something else in mind when he said 'Simply to say of a man "he has character" is not only to say a great deal of him, but to extol him; for that is a rare attribute which calls forth respect towards him and admiration'. And clearly this sense of character is quite distinct from my first non-committal sense; for a man might well exhibit traits like honesty and truthfulness; yet we might still say of him that he had no character. When Pope said that most women have no characters at all, he was not, surely, saying that they were dishonest, selfish, and menda-cious. Presumably he was suggesting that they were fickle, inconstant, and sporadic in conforming to standards because they were so much at the mercy of their moods and inclinations. Or he might have been sug-gesting that they took their standards entirely from their husbands or from the clique in which they happened to collect. We speak of integrity of character. A man who has it is not credited with any definite traits; but the claim is made that, whatever traits he exhibits, there will be some sort of control and consistency in the manner in which he exhibits them. He will not give way to his inclinations, be easily corrupted, or take his colour from his company. Similarly we speak of strength and weakness of character which is a way of measuring the degree to which a person can be sidetracked, tempted, coerced, corrupted, or altered by ridicule. Character-traits, in the first and non-committal sense of character, could be merely the imprint of the social code on a man. Such a man, like the Spartans, could behave consistently in a particular social group; but when he went abroad he would fall an easy victim to the corrupting influence of potentates, priests, and profligates. Or, like Rousseau, without the constraining influence of the General Will, he would be at the mercy of his vacillating inclinations. But a man who has character, in this third sense, would have developed his own distinctive style of rule-following. This would involve consistency and integrity. It is significant that typical descriptions of men of character dwell not so much on the rules which they follow, the particular traits of a substantive sort which they exhibit, but on the manner in which they follow or exhibit them. When we talk of a person's character a trait like honesty springs to mind; but when we speak of a man as having character, it is something like in-tegrity, incorruptibility, or consistency. These descriptions relate to traits

---

[9] I am grateful to Sidney Morgenbesser for pointing this out to me in his com-ments on my paper at the Harvard Conference.

that are necessary conditions of 'having character', but they can apply to different 'types of character' and to a great variety of lower order traits. They describe the style, not the content of a man's rule-following. And though, as Kant points out, to say that a man has character is to praise him, we can say that he has character but that he is bad. Robespierre and the robber-barons had character. Conversely we can often find something to praise even in a consummate villain if we can apply such 'style' descriptions to his behaviour. A Quaker lady was once told that she would find something good to say even about the devil. To which she replied, 'Well, he is persistent.'

It is therefore very important for educators to get clearer about what they have in mind when they speak of 'the training of character'; for it is quite possible for different educators to stress this and to have quite different conceptions of an ideal man. They might all be agreed on the desirability of developing traits like consistency, integrity, and persistence; yet they might disagree vehemently about which substantive traits were desirable as well as about the type of character that was to be encouraged. Quaker educators and supporters of the 'Outward Bound' movement all emphasise the training of character. But they subscribe to very different conceptions of an ideal man. It is therefore necessary to look more carefully into the relationship between types of character and the notion of 'having character'.

Types of Character and 'Having Character'

The analysis of 'having character' already sketched has defined this notion against two main species of 'the heteronomy of the will', to use Kantian language. It rules out, first of all, the man who is at the mercy of his passing inclinations, whose behaviour shows very little sign of being rule-governed. It rules out, secondly, the man whose behaviour is rule-governed, but whose rules are those of the company which he is keeping. Modern typologies of character pick out men such as these. Riesman's anomic, tradition-directed and other-directed types of character spring to mind. Peck and Havighurst speak of amoral and conforming types of character. The former is the psychopathic type who follows his whims and impulses, regulating them only sporadically. The latter is a man who has no generalised or thought-out principles about being e.g. honest. He is often found in stable folk societies and what are called 'shame cultures'. There is, however, an ambiguity about this type of character. For such a man could be one who has no settled principles of his own and who acts *in accordance* with a principle such as 'When in Rome live like the Romans'. Chameleon-like he would adapt himself to any company that he was keeping out of fear or need for approval. But he might also, as a matter of *policy,* act on a principle such as 'One ought always to follow those rules that others follow' or 'One ought always to follow the rules laid down by the Church, the leader or the local community group'. We would say of the former type of con- formist that he had no character. But we might say of the latter that he very definitely had character. Presumably many Jesuits, army officers, and organisation men fall into this latter category. They would really be 'inner-directed men' though their supreme principle would always enjoin them to do what someone else laid down.

Usually, however, men who have character exemplify other types of character distinguished both by Riesman and by Peck and Havig- hurst. Riesman speaks of the 'inner-directed' type of character. Such a man acts consistently on internalised rules. Typically he is a Puritan. His moral philosophy is that of Price's or Sir David Ross' 'intuitionism'. He does what his inner voice tells him that he should even though the heavens fall. He is not, overtly at any rate, swayed by his desires and inclinations; he is impervious to what others think of him and cannot be shamed into conformity. He feels *guilt* only about departing from his inner convictions about what is right. His policies are rigid and, if he is an extreme case of this type of character, he will be a compulsive or an obsessive. But he has character all right. Indeed Sargant in his re- cent book,[10] claimed that such people, together with detached cynics, were the most impervious to systematic brain-washing.

The irrational type of inner-directed character must be distinguished from the more rational type, often called, as by Riesman, the autonomous character. There is, in this type of character, a less rigid type of rule- following; for the rules are applied intelligently and often revised in the light of higher-order principles. If the supreme principle is one such as 'One ought always to further only one's own interests' the man will be what Peck and Havighurst call an expedient type of character. He will be Philip Rieff's interpretation of the Freudian ideal of 'the psy- chological man' of cautious prudence.[11] If, on the other hand, the su- preme principle is 'One ought to consider interests impartially' he will be a Utilitarian, and if it is 'One ought to consider only the interests of others' he will be an altruist. Peck and Havighurst ignore the distinction between these latter two types in the conception of the rational-altruistic type of character. All three types of character are 'inner-directed' and can have character if their behaviour is consistently rule-governed and

---

[10] W. Sargant, *The Battle for the Mind* (Heinemann, Melbourne, 1957).

[11] P. Rieff, *Freud, the Mind of the Moralist* (Viking Press, New York, 1959). Chs. IX and X.

if they adapt their rules intelligently in the light of their supreme principles.

The Complex Task of Moral Education

This analysis, though sketchy, should be sufficient to indicate how complex the business of moral education must be. To simplify the approach to it I propose to use a model, though I am well aware that this, like all such models, fails to fit the phenomena at certain places. Instead of conceiving society, as Plato did, as the individual 'writ large', I propose to conceive of the mind of the individual as a focus of social rules and functions in relation to them. A child, if we are to trust Freud, starts life with a strange amalgam of wishes and mental processes which can scarcely be called thoughts because they do not proceed in accordance with canons of logical or causal connectedness. Wishes become wants when social standards defining ends and efficient and socially appropriate ways of attaining them become imposed on this autistic amalgam. With the development of the 'ego' and 'super-ego' these unruly wishes are regulated, shaped, and transformed by considerations of prudence and social appropriateness. The child's 'character' emerges as the particular style of rule-following which he develops. And there develop, too, further functions in relation to such rules.[12] There will be, in other words, not only rules which govern the behaviour of the individual but there will also be 'writ small' legislative, judicial, and executive functions in relation to them. The following clusters of problems will therefore have to be considered by the educator:

(a) Which rules is it vital for the growing child to absorb? What character is he to have in the first and non-committal sense of 'character'? Next the educator will have to consider what *type* of character should be promoted. This will cover the question of (b) the legislative function, i.e. some procedural principles for modifying and revising rules as well as (c) the question of the judicial function. For the child could learn to apply rules in a rigid rule of thumb manner or could develop discrimination and judgment. Finally the educator will presumably want the child to develop 'character' in the third sense. This will present itself (d) as the problem of developing a stable executive function in the mind of the child.

To discuss moral education within this sort of framework it is necessary to indicate, to start with, the point of view with which one approaches the problem. My concern is for the development of an autono-

[12] See R. S. Peters, *The Concept of Motivation* (Kegan-Paul, London, 1958), pp. 62-71.

mous type of character who follows rules in a rational discriminating manner, and who also has character. To do this a man must subscribe to some higher order principles which will enable him both to apply rules intelligently in the light of relevant differences in circumstances and to revise rules from time to time in the light of changes in circumstances and in empirical knowledge about the consequences of their application. The most important higher order principles which, in my view, are capable of some sort of rational justification, are those of impartiality and the consideration of interests. For these are presupposed in any attempt to justify the rules of practical discourse.[13] These higher order principles, though pretty formal in character, provide a very general criterion of relevance for justifying particular rules and for making exceptions in particular cases. The ideal is that the individual will develop as Kant put it 'as a law-making member of a kingdom of ends'. He must not only come to know what is in general right or wrong; he must also go beyond the level of what Plato called 'ὀρθὴ δόξα,. so that he sees why such rules are right and wrong and can revise rules and make new ones in the light of new knowledge and new circumstances. To do this he must both be introduced to the basic rules of his community and to the higher level principles which enable him to exercise a legislative function.

John Dewey: Ethical Principles Underlying Education[1]

It is commonplace to say that this development of character is the ultimate end of all school work. The difficulty lies in the execution of this idea. And an underlying difficulty in this execution is the lack of any conception of what character means. This may seem an extreme and uncalled-for statement. If so, the idea may be better conveyed by saying that we conceive of character simply in terms of results; that we have no clear conception of it in psychological terms—that is, as a process, as working or dynamic. We know what character means in terms of the kinds of actions which proceed from character, but we have not a definite

---

[13] For attempts towards such a justification see S. I. Benn and R. S. Peters, *Social Principles and the Democratic State* (Allen & Unwin, London, 1959), Ch. 2, A. P. Griffiths, *Justifying Moral Principles,* Proc. Aris. Soc. LVIII, 1957-8, and Sidgwick's discussion of the Principles of Justice, Egoism, and Rational Benevolence in his *Methods of Ethics* (MacMillan, London, 1874).

[1] From John Dewey, *John Dewey on Education—Selected Writings.* New York: The Modern Library, Random House, Inc., 1964, pp. 132-135, with omissions. The article, "Ethical Principles Underlying Education," was originally published in the *Third Yearbook of the National Herbart Society,* 1897.

conception of it on its inner side, as a piece of running, psychical machinery.

I propose, then, to give a brief statement of the nature of character from this point of view. In general, character means power of social agency, organized capacity of social functioning. It means, as already suggested, social insight or intelligence, social executive power, and social interest or responsiveness. Stated in psychological terms, it means that there must be a training of the primary impulses and instincts, which organize them into habits which are reliable means of action.

1. Force, efficiency in execution, or overt action, is the necessary constituent of character. In our moral books and lectures we may lay all the stress upon good intentions, etc. But we know practically that the kind of character we hope to build up through our education is one which not only has good intentions, but which insists upon carrying them out. Any other character is wishy-washy; it is goody, not good. The individual must have the power to stand up and count for something in the actual conflicts of life. He must have initiative, insistence, persistence, courage and industry. He must in a word, have all that goes under a term, "force of character." Undoubtedly, individuals differ greatly in their native endowment in this respect. None the less, each has a certain primary equipment of impulse, of tendency forward, of innate urgency to do. The problem of education on this side is that of discovering what this native fund of power is, and then of utilizing it in such a way (affording conditions which both stimulate and control) as to organize it into definite conserved modes of action—habits.

2. But something more is required than sheer force. Sheer force may be brutal; it may override the interests of others. Even when aiming at right ends it may go at them in such a way as to violate the rights of others. More than this, in sheer force there is no guarantee for the right end itself. It may be directed towards mistaken ends, and result in positive mischief and destruction. Power, as already suggested, must be directed. It must be organized along certain channels of output or expression in such a way as to be attached to the valuable ends.

This involves training on both the intellectual and emotional side. On the intellectual side we must have judgment—what is ordinarily called good sense. The difference between mere knowledge, or information, and judgment is that the former is simply held, not used; judgment is ideas directed with reference to the accomplishment of ends. Good judgment is a sense of respective or proportionate values. The one who has judgment is the one who has ability to size up a situation. He is the one who can grasp the scene or situation before him, ignoring what is irrelevant, or what for the time being is unimportant, and can seize upon the factors which demand attention, and grade them according to their respective claims. Mere knowledge of what the right is in the abstract, mere intentions of following the right in general, however praiseworthy in themselves, are never a substitute for this power of trained judgment. Action is always in the concrete. It is definite and individualized. Except, therefore, as it is backed and controlled by a knowledge of the actual concrete factors in the situation demanding action, it must be relatively futile and waste.

3. But the consciousness of end must be more than merely intellectual. We can imagine a person with most excellent judgment, who yet does not act upon his judgment. There must not only be force to insure effort in execution against obstacles, but there must also be a delicate personal responsiveness—there must be an emotional reaction. Indeed good judgment is impossible without this susceptibility. Unless there is a prompt and almost instinctive sensitiveness to the conditions about one, to the ends and interests of others, the intellectual side of judgment will not have its proper material to work upon. Just as the material of objects of knowledge is related to the senses, so the material of ethical knowledge is related to emotional responsiveness. It is difficult to put this quality into words, but we all know the difference between the character which is somewhat hard and formal, and that which is sympathetic, flexible, and open. In the abstract the former may be as sincerely devoted to moral ideas as the latter, but as a practical matter we prefer to live with the latter, and we count upon it to accomplish more in the end by tact, by instinctive recognition of the claims of others, by skill in adjusting, than the former can accomplish by mere attachment to rules and principles which are intellectually justified.

John Dewey: Theories of Morals[1]

... What is learned and employed in an occupation having an aim and involving coöperation with others is moral knowledge, whether consciously so regarded or not. For it builds up a social interest and confers the intelligence needed to make that interest effective in practice. Just because the studies of the curriculum represent standard factors in social life, they are organs of initiation into social values. As mere school studies, their acquisition has only a technical worth. Acquired under conditions where their social significance is realized, they feed moral

[1] From John Dewey, *Democracy and Education.* New York: The Macmillan Company, Free Press of Glencoe, paperback edition, 1966, pp. 356-360, with omissions. Reprinted by permission of The Macmillan Company, copyright 1916, The Macmillan Company; renewed 1944 by John Dewey.

interest and develop moral insight. Moreover, the qualities of mind discussed under the topic of method of learning are all of them intrinsically
moral qualities. Open-mindedness, single-mindedness, sincerity, breadth
of outlook, thoroughness, assumption of responsibility for developing
the consequences of ideas which are accepted, are moral traits. The habit
of identifying moral characteristics with external conformity to authoritative prescriptions may lead us to ignore the ethical value of these intellectual attitudes, but the same habit tends to reduce morals to a dead
and machine-like routine. Consequently while such an attitude has
moral results, the results are morally undesirable—above all in a democratic society where so much depends upon personal disposition.

The Social and the Moral.   All of the separations which we have
been criticizing—and which the idea of education set forth in the previous chapters is designed to avoid—spring from taking morals too
narrowly, giving them, on one side, a sentimental goody-goody turn
without reference to effective ability to do what is socially needed, and,
on the other side, overemphasizing convention and tradition so as to
limit morals to a list of definitely stated acts. As a matter of fact, morals
are as broad as acts which concern our relationships with others. And
potentially this includes all our acts, even though their social bearing
may not be thought of at the time of performance. For every act, by the
principle of habit, modifies disposition—it sets up a certain kind of inclination and desire. And it is impossible to tell when the habit thus
strengthened may have a direct and perceptible influence on our association with others. Certain traits of character have such an obvious connection with our social relationships that we call them "moral" in an
emphatic sense—truthfulness, honesty, chastity, amiability, etc. But this
only means that they are, as compared with some other attitudes, central
—that they carry other attitudes with them. They are moral in an emphatic sense not because they are isolated and exclusive, but because
they are so intimately connected with thousands of other attitudes which
we do not explicitly recognize—which perhaps we have not even names
for. To call them virtues in their isolation is like taking the skeleton for
the living body. The bones are certainly important, but their importance
lies in the fact that they support other organs of the body in such a way
as to make them capable of effective integrated activity. And the same
is true of the qualities of character which we specifically designate virtues. Morals concern nothing less than the whole character, and the
whole character is identical with the man in all his concrete make-up
and manifestations. To possess virtue does not signify to have cultivated
a few nameable and exclusive traits; it means to be fully and adequately

what one is capable of becoming through association with others in all the offices of life.

The moral and the social quality of conduct are, in the last analysis, identical with each other. It is then but to restate explicitly the import of our earlier chapters regarding the social function of education to say that the measure of the worth of the administration, curriculum, and methods of instruction of the school is the extent to which they are animated by a social spirit. And the great danger which threatens school work is the absence of conditions which makes possible a permeating social spirit; this is the great enemy of effective moral training. For this spirit can be actively present only when certain conditions are met.

(*i*) In the first place, the school must itself be a community life in all which that implies. Social perceptions and interests can be developed only in a genuinely social medium—one where there is give and take in the building up of a common experience. Informational statements about things can be acquired in relative isolation by any one who previously has had enough intercourse with others to have learned language. But realization of the *meaning* of the linguistic signs is quite another matter. That involves a context of work and play in association with others. The plea which has been made for education through continued constructive activities in this book rests upon the fact they afford an opportunity for a social atmosphere. In place of a school set apart from life as a place for learning lessons, we have a miniature social group in which study and growth are incidents of present shared experience. Playgrounds, shops, workrooms, laboratories not only direct the natural active tendencies of youth, but they involve intercourse, communication, and coöperation,—all extending the perception of connections.

(*ii*) The learning in school should be continuous with that out of school. There should be a free interplay between the two. This is possible only when there are numerous points of contact between the social interests of the one and of the other. A school is conceivable in which there should be a spirit of companionship and shared activity, but where its social life would no more represent or typify that of the world beyond the school walls than that of a monastery. Social concern and understanding would be developed, but they would not be available outside; they would not carry over. The proverbial separation of town and gown, the cultivation of academic seclusion, operates in this direction. So does such adherence to the culture of the past as generates a reminiscent social spirit, for this makes an individual feel more at home in the life of other days than in his own. A professedly cultural education is peculiarly exposed to this danger. An idealized past becomes the refuge and solace of the spirit; present-day concerns are found sordid, and unworthy of attention. But as a rule, the absence of a social environment in connection with which learning is a need and a reward is the chief reason for the isolation of the school; and this isolation renders school knowledge inapplicable to life and so infertile in character.

A narrow and moralistic view of morals is responsible for the failure to recognize that all the aims and values which are desirable in education are themselves moral. Discipline, natural development, culture, social efficiency, are moral traits—marks of a person who is a worthy member of that society which it is the business of education to further. There is an old saying to the effect that it is not enough for a man to be good; he must be good for something. The something for which a man must be good is capacity to live as a social member so that what he gets from living with others balances with what he contributes. What he gets and gives as a human being, a being with desires, emotions, and ideas, is not external possessions, but a widening and deepening of conscious life— a more intense, disciplined, and expanding realization of meanings. What he *materially* receives and gives is at most opportunities and means for the evolution of conscious life. Otherwise, it is neither giving nor taking, but a shifting about of the position of things in space, like the stirring of water and sand with a stick. Discipline, culture, social efficiency, personal refinement, improvement of character are but phases of the growth of capacity nobly to share in such a balanced experience. And education is not a mere means to such a life. Education is such a life. To maintain capacity for such education is the essence of morals. For conscious life is a continual beginning afresh.

Summary.   The most important problem of moral education in the school concerns the relationship of knowledge and conduct. For unless the learning which accrues in the regular course of study affects character, it is futile to conceive the moral end as the unifying and culminating end of education. When there is no intimate organic connection between the methods and materials of knowledge and moral growth, particular lessons and modes of discipline have to be resorted to: knowledge is not integrated into the usual springs of action and the outlook on life, while morals become moralistic—a scheme of separate virtues.

The two theories chiefly associated with the separation of learning from activity, and hence from morals, are those which cut off inner disposition and motive—the conscious personal factor—and deeds as purely physical and outer; and which set action from interest in opposition to that from principle. Both of these separations are overcome in an educational scheme where learning is the accompaniment of continuous activities or occupations which have a social aim and utilize the materials of typical social situations. For under such conditions, the school becomes itself a form of social life, a miniature community and one in close interaction with other modes of associated experience beyond school walls. All education which develops power to share effectively in social life is moral. It forms a character which not only does the particular deed socially necessary but one which is interested in that continuous readjustment which is essential to growth. Interest in learning from all the contacts of life is the essential moral interest.

Personal ends-in-view

5

Self-Made Goals

Parts I and II of this anthology illustrated educational ends-in-view as they are often prescribed by an educationist or educator *for* a learning subject. This external relation of aim to learner may have a normative source—someone believing that the learner *ought* to have certain ends-in-view—or it may occur out of a scientific-logical impulse to collect, identify, and classify the educational aims already prescribed by others. The ends-in-view of Part III are no longer external in orientation. Instead they share a common emphasis on principles of individual choice and self-orientation.

Already it has been found that the affective element of complex dispositional objectives requires for its fulfillment a reorientation from public to private, the initiative being transferred from the external author of the disposition to the learner himself. In a general sense, then, the ends-in-view of the last chapter are related to those of the present. In a particular sense, however, the first selection of this chapter is an answer to the two preceding selections from Dewey. For although Dewey bases his ends-in-view on concepts of freedom of interaction among and between groups, the dispositions to be formed for social amelioration are *prescribed* dispositions. In other words, the individual is not to be the author of his own dispositions. The emphasis will now be on the self-initiation of goals, and in the following chapter on the possibility of goals being initiated by groups.

Although public and private ends-in-view are opposed by placement in separate parts of this anthology, the interplay in experience between externally prescribed ends-in-view and private ends-in-view, or goals, is continuous and varied in a manner suggested in Chapter 1. The individual may be the author of his own goals or they may be appropriated from others. Ideals, on the one hand, and simple and complex objectives on the other, may each become goals by this process of appropriation and personal assimilation.

In the process of teacher-pupil interaction, public and private ends-in-view may be related in a variety of ways. To illustrate: (a) a student may impose upon himself the task of learning a theorem, or certain French verbs *before* this simple goal becomes a teacher-directed, "public" objective for him and his fellows; (b) the teacher may first formulate the objective for his students and successfully transfer it to a particular one as a willingly accepted goal; (c) in some cases the simple goal and the simple objective may happen to be initiated simultaneously by both student and teacher. The need for improved spelling competence may be realized by both as the teacher is correcting orally a class spelling test; (d) the student's simple goal and the teacher's simple objective may be initiated simultaneously, as in (c), and pursued for a period in parallel but interacting and mutually sustaining ways, as when a teacher produces a class play or a choir-master prepares a madrigal group for a public performance.

Some student goals are vocational. Of these, some may be dreamstates pitched well beyond the capacities of the individual, and for that reason may conflict with the objectives a teacher may have for the student. Others may be only vaguely and intermittently perceived, and though achievable, not seriously pursued, and not in serious competition with a teacher's objectives. Some may be achievable, clearly perceived, and pursued with constant determination—often in harmony with a teacher's objectives. Whatever their type, private character goals are rarely articulated.

The initial selection by Morris is introductory, presenting an Existentialist viewpoint on education. As such it contrasts with all external formulations of educational aims in so far as each of these is intended as a design for others. As an Existentialist statement, the first selection has some affinity with Buber's earlier argument that every individual is a human subject in his own right, to be restored to full responsibility for his own self. It is related also (although less closely) to Nunn's ideal of human individuality in Chapter 1, section 1.

Morris reiterates the common Existentialist emphases on subjectivity, on the need for awareness of individual freedom of choice in respect to values, and on the need for the individual, by his own acts of responsible choice, to make something of himself, to create his own "essence." Educational ends-in-view become reoriented. The young are not things to be manipulated by patronizing adults; they are subjects, and the choice of what they are to make of their own lives is to be theirs. Theirs too is to be the responsibility for their choices, for the best disposition, by implication, is a disinclination to be puppets of others in questions of values. Many have reached a similar aversion to externally imposed aims of education without the "aegis of Existentialism," and a similar opposition to Dewey's "public criterion" in what appears to them to be a presumption in anyone who strives to make something of others' lives. Morris's contribution is pertinent to the topic of self-made goals for its accent on the principle of personal choice.

Something of this challenge to the individual to be what he wants himself to be, and something of the very "courage to be" itself, are suggested in the autobiographical selections that follow. However, although autobiographies are the most credible source of such aims, their veracity is liable to be influenced by the writer's motives. The autobiographical selections are offered, therefore, in full awareness both of the difficulty of ascertaining truth and of the lapses to which memory is prone.

In marked contrast to all external aims that remain unassimilated or partially assimilated by the learner, personal aims are dynamic and practical and are based on an individual's desire to make something of himself by his own decisions and efforts. Because societies find it proper to impose educational aims on children, personal educational aims are often formed in post-school years. Thus in the second selection, Charles Darwin shows how his own educational goals were influenced by the interplay of fortuitous circumstances and natural endowment and temperament. In the third selection, Churchill first exposes the purposelessness and frustration he experienced in his schooling at Harrow, with its subjection of pupils to externally formulated ideals and objectives. He then states, in contrast, the educational goals he set for himself out of the impulse to change his comparative lack of knowledge, in an effort to remove the stigma of ignorance.

In a sense, both Darwin and Churchill appear to vindicate Morris's plea for personal choice and responsibility. Each has the freshness and zest of an explorer, free to set his own compass. But now a foil is introduced. The heavy moralizing hand of Pillans—true to his age—is laid over a whole people as he prescribes an education deemed suitable for the youth of Britain in 1835. By contrast with the preceding spontaneity, lightness, and authenticity, Pillans is pompous, leaden, austere, and as confident as an old-fashioned schoolmaster who believes that he alone knows what is best for his charges. Ironically, he speaks on liberal education, and, ironically too, the spirit of imposition which he expresses is perennial, alive among well-intentioned educators of every age.

Van Cleve Morris: An Educational Theory[1]

It is a convention in the craft that every philosophy is expected to concoct and offer up a grand, plenary, umbrella-like phrase under which all lesser educational ideas are to be classified and understood. The world of educational philosophy has its full share of these final, all-embracing rubrics.

One of the oldest and still the most popular is the notion that education is the drawing out of our common human nature. The Aristotelian Rational Humanists and the Neo-Thomists in general, and Robert Hutchins and Mortimer Adler in particular, have made this a virtual byword slogan in twentieth-century educational philosophy. Working from a supposed etymological root of the word "education" in the Latin *educere*, "to lead out," they insist that all education is a process of summoning forth prior but only incipient elements in the child's nature. As it happens, there is considerable disagreement about this etymology among Latin scholars; some claim that "education" comes from *educare*, "to rear or nurture." Although the latter view might provide the base for a differently oriented definition, in either case education is thought of as working with what is already given in the child's nature.

A somewhat less sophisticated and more prosaic definition of education is the taking on, or the "taking *in*," of the accumulated and stored-up knowledge and wisdom of the race. This view, generally attributed to those who call themselves Essentialists, has been espoused by the late William C. Bagley and the contemporary Clifton Hall. The child is a passive element in a process by which he receives, absorbs, and assimilates the various arts and sciences of civilization. Professor Hall speaks of it as "furnishing the mind," an expression intended, I think, to call forward the analogy of furnishing an apartment. No prior nature is postulated except the capacity (the "container" metaphor is intentional) to receive and be the receptacle for as much of the world's knowledge as possible, and, of course, in the process to develop the major skills of reading, writing, and calculating upon which all such learning depends.

According to a third definition, more nearly tuned to the behavioral sciences of the twentieth century and developed with some force by such individuals as George Counts and John Childs, education is the shaping of individuals—their understandings, their attitudes, their values and

[1]"Does Education Have a Definition?" From Van Cleve Morris, *Existentialism in Education*. New York: Harper & Row, Publishers, 1966, pp. 105-111. Copyright 1966 by Van Cleve Morris. Reprinted by permission of Harper & Row, Publishers.

aspirations—in terms of the culture in which they happen to live. Here the assimilation of the arts and sciences of civilization is taken for granted. But which arts? Which sciences? The *use* to which the arts and sciences shall be put is always determined by a culture existing at a specific time in history and a specific place in the world's political geography. Hence, the *value* of this or that art or science is always a function of the social system at a given time in its history. Thus, whether or not a particular art or science is to be taught or learned is a negotiable matter to be determined in light of the culture's own ethic. As the famous epigram has it, whatever a culture values, that will it teach to its young. And that will its young become.

Finally, we may draw upon an even more general definition offered a half-century ago by John Dewey, a definition which does, in a sense, rationalize and make comprehensible all definitions of education which issue from philosophical origins. In a passage probably quoted more frequently than any other, especially by educational philosophers in justifying what they do for a living, Professor Dewey epitomizes the vital link between education and philosophy: "If we are willing to conceive education as the process of forming fundamental dispositions, intellectual and emotional, toward nature and fellow men, philosophy may even be defined *as the general theory of education.*"

The latter portion of this passage has been worried over in endless commentaries in the field of philosophy of education. There is no need to discuss it further. Rather, I wish to draw attention to the definition of education made explicit in the first clause: "the process of forming fundamental dispositions." This is sufficiently straightforward not to require any labored exegesis, but perhaps a small gloss might be offered for it: Dewey is saying that human beings have dispositions ("intellectual and emotional, toward nature and fellow men"), that some of these dispositions are fundamental, that it is conceivable and possible to form them in young people by deliberate, intentional, and premeditated means, and that this activity we shall call by the name education.

Now, precisely what does it signify to speak of a disposition as being "fundamental"? Although there may be no strict logical entailment in such an equivalence, I think Dewey is clearly trying to intimate that whatever is fundamental is somehow desirable and worth pursuing in the process of "forming." He has given a kind of heuristic assignment to the word "fundamental" by which he implies that the dispositions to be formed are not only fundamental but of considerable interest to us; they are important to the task of giving a young person's developing life a focus and an orientation necessary for happiness and success. In short, we very much *want* youngsters to possess these dispositions.

Are we reading too much into the definition? I think not. A few pages prior to the passage quoted, Dewey speaks of the role of philosophy as "thinking what the known demands of us—what responsive attitude it exacts." And when he marries philosophy to education, it is clear that he expects some responsive attitudes to turn out to be of higher rank or of more lasting value than others. These are the attitudes to be formed.

To thus paraphrase Dewey does not mean to suggest that he is ignoring the important role of the learner. Indeed, most of Dewey's writing in education served to explain how this role could become far more active and constructive than any previous theory had conceived it. Not only was the child a participant in the "forming" activity but, through his own experience and the "feedback" effect of his reaction to the dispositions made available to him, the learner shared in deciding what dispositions were most worth forming in his own character. The fact remains, however, that the dispositions finally decided upon were not of his own unique authorship; they were always the dispositions that had been worked out in company with others. Hence, in the end, the learner discovered that he did not need to take *personal* responsibility for having selected them as the dispositions most suited to his own life. They were the dispositions worked out and certified by the group. They were not *his*.

One of the dispositions on which Dewey put a high value was the disposition to *share*. The sharing of information, the sharing of experiences, the sharing of viewpoints and opinions, the sharing of cooperative help in the working out of learning projects—all these were considered good, and the disposition to share with one's fellows came to have an overpowering importance in Dewey's educational theory. Inevitably, the "morality of sharing" places a high premium on human intercourse and personal gregariousness. Gregariousness, then, came to assume a large auxiliary function in support of the sharing disposition. It is partly for this reason that, under Dewey's influence and that of the Progressives over the last fifty years, the *socialization* of the child has come into equal prominence with the *intellectual development* of the child as a strategic educational aim.

Now, here we have, from a variety that might have been cited, four representative and widely held definitions of education. The reader of this book should have no trouble detecting the flaw they all contain so far as an Existentialist educator might be concerned. Education may be all of these things superficially, he would say, but each viewpoint makes the same mistake, the mistake of believing that the young are *things* to be worked over in some fashion to bring them into alignment with a prior notion of what they *should* be. The young, in these conceptions of education, are to be *used;* they are to be employed on behalf of (1) a prepared, precertified idea of "human nature" which they are expected to fulfill, (2) an objective body of extant subject matter which they are expected to absorb, (3) an objective concept of a culture's ways and means of living which they are expected to assume, or (4) a set of dispositions, deemed fundamental, which are to be formed in them and for which they are expected to become the living vehicles.

In every case the process of education is understood to have its aim and point *outside* the learner. The child, by virtue of what is to be done with him and for him, is eventually seen as an object rather than a subject. His activity of learning is aroused and promoted in the name of considerations residing outside his own self-determination and self-direction.

I am not so naïve as to think that this charge will go unchallenged by Experimentalists and Progressives. As everyone knows, they claim to have succeeded, where earlier theories had not, in bringing the learner at last into a self-determining posture. It may come as some surprise to them, therefore, to hear someone say that they have failed to deliver on this pledge. But that is precisely what I am prepared to assert.

We have hinted at the difficulty in the paragraphs above dealing with Dewey's conception of education as "the forming of fundamental dispositions." Even if the child is a participant in the forming process, and even if he is in a cybernetic way always helping to decide what dispositions are most worth forming, it is still true in Experimentalist theory that the criterion he uses for judging one disposition against another will be a *public* rather than a personal and private criterion. That is to say, whether a disposition measures up as worthy of adoption will always be decided in terms of whether it will aid the individual in his present and future existence *with* and *among* other people. Under the aegis of an unspoken, virtually iron law of Experimentalist moral theory, a *public* criterion will always, in the last analysis, outrank and overpower a purely *private* criterion as to how life is to be looked at and lived.

I think we can see in the previously mentioned "uncoerced community of persuasion" the clue to the Achilles' heel of Experimentalist doctrine. The key word in this well-known phrase is *community*. Here, I think it not unfair to say, the Experimentalist finally rests his case. The *community* dimension to the Experimentalist's logic, to his method of inquiry, to his moral theory is the final, unarguable principle. As an article of doctrine, if not of faith, it is the ultimate canon which is not negotiable. If the test of the truth of an idea lies in its effects, these effects are understood to be *public* effects; if the test of a moral prescription lies in its consequences, these consequences are understood to be *public* consequences. Public effects and public consequences are the only kinds that can be useful to science. In the social sciences especially we see this requirement most vividly. Without public, repeatable phenomena, the social scientist's data would mean nothing. His data are, by definition, the data of purely public events.

It should surprise no one, then, that an Experimentalist's education has to be oriented to the public, community criterion. What is to be learned, how it is to be learned, how the learning of it is to be adjudged successful or unsuccessful—all these have their determination against a social measure. If this or that learning experience is made available to a youngster, in the final analysis its importance in his learning career will be argued for in terms of what it can mean for him in the *world of others*. What that experience may mean to him for purely private consumption will possibly intrude as an ancillary note, but in Experimentalist educational theory such a consideration is always, and indeed must be, subordinate.

In light of the foregoing argument we can see a disturbing truth, namely, that an Experimentalist definition of education eventually falters, like all the others, in its attempt to bring the learner's own self-determination to the very center of the learning process. And it is precisely this that Existentialism claims to do.

Does Existentialism have a definition of education? I am not so sure. There is a certain wariness of definitions in such a philosophy. Yet there is at least the possibility that something comprehensible can be put into words to typify the Existentialist's stance vis-à-vis the educative process. He might say something like this: If education is to be truly human, it must somehow *awaken awareness* in the learner—existential awareness of himself as a single subjectivity present in the world.

To be human is first to exist, and to exist is to be aware of being, to be aware of existing. This awareness is manifest most vividly, as we have said, in the awareness of choosing, the sometimes painful, sometimes exhilarating awareness of oneself as a baseless base of value creation. Is this "awareness," someone might ask, another of those "fundamental dispositions" which were just put aside a few pages back? The answer must be "No." How can awareness be a disposition? To be aware is not to be disposed this way or that. It is, rather, to be aware of the *possibility* of being disposed this way or that. *It is to be aware that one is the author of his own dispositions!*

To be disposed to sharing, one must *choose* to be so disposed. To be gregarious, one must individually *choose* gregariousness. To permit a public criterion to monitor how one looks at life, one must privately *choose* to consent to that criterion. An education which reminds youngsters that they are constantly, freely, baselessly, creatively choosing in this way is the kind of education we are in pursuit of. It is the education of private awareness and personal involvement.

Charles Darwin: Autobiography[1]

During my second year in Edinburgh I attended Jameson's lectures on Geology and Zoology, but they were incredibly dull. The sole effect they produced on me was the determination never as long as I lived to read a book on Geology or in any way to study the science. Yet I feel sure that I was prepared for a philosophical treatment of the subject; for an old Mr. Cotton in Shropshire who knew a good deal about rocks, had pointed out to me, two or three years previously a well-known large erratic boulder in the town of Shrewsbury, called the bell-stone; he told me that there was no rock of the same kind nearer than Cumberland or Scotland, and he solemnly assured me that the world would come to an end before anyone would be able to explain how this stone came where it now lay. This produced a deep impression on me and I meditated over this wonderful stone. So that I felt the keenest delight when I first read of the action of icebergs in transporting boulders, and I gloried in the progress of Geology. Equally striking is the fact that I, though now only sixty-seven years old, heard Professor Jameson, in a field lecture at Salisbury Craigs, discoursing on a trap-dyke, with amygdaloidal margins and the strata indurated on each side, with volcanic rocks all around us, and say that it was a fissure filled with sediment from above, adding with a sneer that there were men who maintained that it had been injected from beneath in a molten condition. When I think of this lecture, I do not wonder that I determined never to attend to Geology.

From attending Jameson's lectures, I became acquainted with the curator of the museum, Mr. Macgillivray, who afterwards published a large and excellent book on the birds of Scotland. He had not much the appearance or manners of the gentleman. I had much interesting natural-history talk with him, and he was very kind to me. He gave me some rare shells, for I at that time collected marine mollusca, but with no great zeal.

*   *   *   *

But no pursuit at Cambridge was followed with nearly so much eagerness or gave me so much pleasure as collecting beetles. It was the

[1]From Nora Barlow, (ed.), *The Autobiography of Charles Darwin, 1802-1882.* London: William Collins, Sons and Co., 1958, pp. 52-53, 62-63, with omissions. Reprinted by permission of A. D. Peters & Co., and Harcourt, Brace & World, Inc.

mere passion for collecting, for I did not dissect them and rarely compared their external characters with published descriptions, but got them named anyhow. I will give a proof of my zeal: one day, on tearing off some old bark, I saw two rare beetles and seized one in each hand; then I saw a third and new kind, which I could not bear to lose, so that I popped the one which I held in my right hand into my mouth. Alas it ejected some intensely acrid fluid, which burnt my tongue so that I was forced to spit the beetle out, which was lost, as well as the third one.

I was very successful in collecting and invented two new methods; I employed a labourer to scrape during the winter, moss off old trees and place [it] in a large bag, and likewise to collect the rubbish at the bottom of the barges in which reeds are brought from the fens, and thus I got some very rare species. No poet ever felt more delight at seeing his first poem published than I did at seeing in Stephen's *Illustrations of British Insects* the magic words, "captured by C. Darwin, Esq." I was introduced to entomology by my second cousin, W. Darwin Fox, a clever and most pleasant man, who was then at Christ's College, and with whom I became extremely intimate. Afterwards I became well acquainted with and went out collecting, with Albert Way of Trinity, who in after years became a well-known archæologist; also with H. Thompson, of the same College, afterwards a leading agriculturist, chairman of a great Railway, and Member of Parliament. It seems therefore that a taste for collecting beetles is some indication of future success in life!

Winston S. Churchill: Examinations and Education at Bangalore[1]

My stay at the Royal Military College formed an intermediate period in my life. It brought to a close nearly 12 years of school. Thirty-six terms each of many weeks (interspersed with all-too-short holidays) during the whole of which I had enjoyed few gleams of success, in which I had hardly ever been asked to learn anything which seemed of the slightest use or interest, or allowed to play any game which was amusing. In retrospect these years form not only the least agreeable, but the only barren and unhappy period of my life. I was happy as a child with my toys in my nursery. I have been happier every year since I became a man. But this interlude of school makes a sombre grey patch upon the chart of my journey. It was an unending spell of worries that did not

[1] From Winston Churchill, *My Early Life*. London: The Reprint Society, 1944, pp. 46-47, 118-122, with omissions. Reprinted by permission of The Hamlyn Publishing Group Ltd., and Charles Scribner's Sons. Copyright 1930 by Charles Scribner's Sons; renewal copyright 1958 Winston Churchill.

then seem petty, and of toil uncheered by fruition; a time of discomfort, restriction and purposeless monotony.

This train of thought must not lead me to exaggerate the character of my school days. Actually no doubt they were buoyed up by the laughter and high spirits of youth. Harrow was a very good school, and a high standard of personal service prevailed among its masters. Most of the boys were very happy, and many found in its classrooms and upon its playing-fields the greatest distinction they have ever known in life. I can only record the fact that, no doubt through my own shortcomings, I was an exception. I would far rather have been apprenticed as a brick-layer's mate, or run errands as a messenger boy, or helped my father to dress the front windows of a grocer's shop. It would have been real; it would have been natural; it would have taught me more; and I should have done it much better. Also I should have got to know my father, which would have been a joy to me.

Certainly the prolonged education indispensable to the progress of Society is not natural to mankind. It cuts against the grain. A boy would like to follow his father in pursuit of food or prey. He would like to be doing serviceable things so far as his utmost strength allowed. He would like to be earning wages however small to help to keep up the home. He would like to have some leisure of his own to use or mis-use as he pleased. He would ask little more than the right to work or starve. And then perhaps in the evenings a real love of learning would come to those who were worthy—and why try to stuff it into those who are not?—and knowledge and thought would open the 'magic case-ments' of the mind.

I was on the whole considerably discouraged by my school days. Except in Fencing, in which I had won the Public School Championship, I had achieved no distinction. All my contemporaries and even younger boys seemed in every way better adapted to the conditions of our little world. They were far better both at the games and at the lessons. It is not pleasant to feel oneself so completely outclassed and left behind at the very beginning of the race. I had been surprised on taking leave of Mr. Welldon to hear him predict, with a confidence for which I could see no foundation, that I should be able to make my way all right. I have always been very grateful to him for this.

I am all for the Public Schools but I do not want to go there again.

*   *   *   *

It was not until this winter of 1896, when I had almost completed my twenty-second year, that the desire for learning came upon me. I began to feel myself wanting in even the vaguest knowledge about many large spheres of thought. I had picked up a wide vocabulary and had a liking for words and for the feel of words fitting and falling into their places like pennies in the slot. I caught myself using a good many words the meaning of which I could not define precisely. I admired these words, but was afraid to use them for fear of being absurd. One day, before I left England, a friend of mine had said: 'Christ's gospel was the last word in Ethics.' This sounded good; but what were Ethics? They had never been mentioned to me at Harrow or Sandhurst. Judging from the context I thought they must mean 'the public school spirit', 'playing the game', *'esprit de corps'*, 'honourable behavior', 'patriotism', and the like. Then someone told me that Ethics were concerned not merely with the things you ought to do, but with why you ought to do them, and that there were whole books written on the subject. I would have paid some scholar £2 at least to give me a lecture of an hour or an hour and a half about Ethics. What was the scope of the subject; what were its main branches; what were the principal questions dealt with, and the chief controversies open; who were the high authorities and which were the standard books? But here in Bangalore there was no one to tell me about Ethics for love or money. Of tactics I had a grip: on politics I had a view: but a concise compendious outline of Ethics was a novelty not to be locally obtained.

This was only typical of a dozen similar mental needs that now began to press insistently upon me. I knew of course that the youths at the Universities were stuffed with all this patter at nineteen and twenty, and could pose you entrapping questions or give baffling answers. We never set much store by them or their affected superiority, remembering that they were only at their books, while we were commanding men and guarding the Empire. Nevertheless I had sometimes resented the apt and copious information which some of them seemed to possess, and I now wished I could find a competent teacher whom I could listen to and cross-examine for an hour or so every day.

Then someone had used the phrase 'the Socratic method'. What was that? It was apparently a way of giving your friend his head in an argument and progging him into a pit by cunning questions. Who was Socrates, anyhow? A very argumentative Greek who had a nagging wife and was finally compelled to commit suicide because he was a nuisance! Still, he was beyond doubt a considerable person. He counted for a lot in the minds of learned people. I wanted 'the Socrates story'. Why had his fame lasted through all the ages? What were the stresses which had led a government to put him to death merely because of the things he said? Dire stresses they must have been: the life of the Athenian Executive or the life of this talkative professor! Such antagonisms do not spring from petty issues. Evidently Socrates had called something into being long ago which was very explosive. Intellectual dynamite! A moral bomb! But there was nothing about it in The Queen's Regulations.

Then there was history. I had always liked history at school. But there we were given only the dullest, driest pemmicanized forms like *The Student's Hume*. Once I had a hundred pages of *The Student's Hume* as a holiday task. Quite unexpectedly, before I went back to school, my father set out to examine me upon it. The period was Charles I. He asked me about the Grand Remonstrance; what did I know about that? I said that in the end the Parliament beat the King and cut his head off. This seemed to me the grandest remonstrance imaginable. It was no good. 'Here,' said my father, 'is a grave parliamentary question affecting the whole structure of our constitutional history, lying near the centre of the task you have been set, and you do not in the slightest degree appreciate the issues involved.' I was puzzled by his concern; I could not see at the time why it should matter so much. Now I wanted to know more about it.

So I resolved to read history, philosophy, economics, and things like that; and I wrote to my mother asking for such books as I had heard of on these topics. She responded with alacrity, and every month the mail brought me a substantial package of what I thought were standard works. In history I decided to begin with Gibbon. Someone had told me that my father had read Gibbon with delight; that he knew whole pages of it by heart, and that it had greatly affected his style of speech and writing. So without more ado I set out upon the eight volumes of Dean Milman's edition of Gibbon's *Decline and Fall of the Roman Empire*. I was immediately dominated both by the story and the style. All through the long glistening middle hours of the Indian day, from when we quitted stables till the evening shadows proclaimed the hour of Polo, I devoured Gibbon. I rode triumphantly through it from end to end and enjoyed it all. I scribbled all my opinions on the margins of the pages, and very soon found myself a vehement partisan of the author against the disparagements of his pompous-pious editor. I was not even estranged by his naughty footnotes. On the other hand the Dean's apologies and disclaimers roused my ire. So pleased was I with *The Decline and Fall* that I began at once to read Gibbon's Autobiography, which luckily was bound up in the same edition. When I read his reference to his old nurse: 'If there be any, as I trust there are some, who rejoice that I live, to that dear and excellent woman their gratitude is due', I thought of Mrs. Everest; and it shall be her epitaph.

From Gibbon I went to Macaulay. I had learnt the *Lays of Ancient Rome* by heart, and loved them; and of course I knew he had written a history; but I had never read a page of it. I now embarked on that splendid romance, and I voyaged with full sail in a strong wind. I remembered then that Mrs. Everest's brother-in-law, the old prison warder, had possessed a copy of Macaulay's History, purchased in supplements and bound together, and that he used to speak of it with reverence. I accepted all Macaulay wrote as gospel, and I was grieved to read his harsh judgments upon the Great Duke of Marlborough. There was no one at hand to tell me that this historian with his captivating style and devastating self-confidence was the prince of literary rogues, who always preferred the tale to the truth, and smirched or glorified great men and garbled documents according as they affected his drama. I cannot forgive him for imposing on my confidence and on the simple faith of my old friend the warder. Still I must admit an immense debt upon the other side.

Not less than in his History, I revelled in his Essays: Chatham; Frederick the Great; Lord Nugent's Memorials of Hampden; Clive; Warren Hastings; Barère (the dirty dog); Southey's Colloquies on Society; and above all that masterpiece of literary ferocity, Mr. Robert Montgomery's Poems.

From November to May I read for four or five hours every day history and philosophy. Plato's Republic—it appeared he was for all practical purposes the same as Socrates; the Politics of Aristotle, edited by Mr. Welldon himself; Schopenhauer on Pessimism; Malthus on Population; Darwin's Origin of Species: all interspersed with other books of lesser standing. It was a curious education. First because I approached it with an empty, hungry mind, and with fairly strong jaws; and what I got I bit; secondly because I had no one to tell me: 'This is discredited'. 'You should read the answer to that by so and so; the two together will give you the gist of the argument'. 'There is a much better book on that subject', and so forth. I now began for the first time to envy those young cubs at the University who had fine scholars to tell them what was what; professors who had devoted their lives to mastering and focussing ideas in every branch of learning; who were eager to distribute the treasures they had gathered before they were overtaken by the night. But now I pity undergraduates, when I see what frivolous lives many of them lead in the midst of precious fleeting opportunity. After all, a man's Life must be nailed to a cross either of Thought or Action. Without work there is no play.

When I am in the Socratic mood and planning *my* Republic, I make drastic changes in the education of the sons of well-to-do citizens. When they are sixteen or seventeen they begin to learn a craft and to do healthy manual labour, with plenty of poetry, songs, dancing, drill and gymnastics in their spare time. They can thus let off their steam on something

useful. It is only when they are really thirsty for knowledge, longing to
hear about things, that I would let them go to the University. It would
be a favour, a coveted privilege, only to be given to those who had either
proved their worth in factory or field or whose qualities and zeal were
pre-eminent. However, this would upset a lot of things; it would cause
commotion and bring me perhaps in the end a hemlock draught.

*   *   *   *

Professor Pillans: On the Proper Objects and Methods of Education[1]

In proceeding to speak of the education required for the higher
classes, as distinguished from that which it is proposed to bring within
the reach of all, it will be proper in the outset to consider well, wherein
the distinction consists between these two kinds of instruction—that
which befits the great mass of working population, and that
which is best adapted for the few. This it is the more necessary to do,
as much of the plausible speculation which has misled the public mind,
is indebted for its effect to the wilful or ignorant confounding of this
very obvious distinction.

It is now-a-days almost universally admitted, that there is an early
training, moral and intellectual, which it is desirable to secure to the
great body of the people, whether agricultural or manufacturing. Now,
it is abundantly obvious, that the object to be kept in view in such early
tuition is, to take advantage of the brief period of docility which intervenes between the age of helpless infancy and that period of life when
the sinews are sufficiently knit for hard and continuous labour, and when
the profit of the child's handiwork becomes available for the support of
the parent, or for its own. This interval, so precious because so brief,
amounts often, in large manufacturing towns, to not more than a single
twelvemonth, and almost everywhere it is a period of lax and irregular
attendance; and yet it is all the time that can be depended upon for training the children of the working classes to such habits, tastes, and feelings,
as may render them honest, industrious, intelligent, and happy. This end,
it is equally clear, will have the best chance of being attained in their
case, by presenting knowledge in an easy and attractive form; by invest-
ing school with pleasant associations and endearing recollections; by im-

[1] From Professor Pillans, *Three Lectures on the Proper Objects and Methods of
Education in Reference to the Different Orders of Society.* Edinburgh:
Maclachlan & Stewart, 2nd edition, 1854. These lectures were delivered in
1835.

parting, in short, not merely the ability to read, but the love of reading and the desire of instruction, so as to furnish the means of filling up, usefully and agreeably, the short respites from toil that occur in the poor man's life.

As means to this end, one can scarcely overrate the importance of Infant Schools. They extend the brief and precious interval just spoken of, by the addition of a still earlier and more susceptible age, during which habits may be formed which will far more than double the benefit to be derived from the later portion of the child's disposable time. And when that still more important improvement shall be introduced, of having public accredited means of training schoolmasters to the skilful discharge of their professional duties—an improvement not altogether so distant and hopeless as it once appeared—it is not easy to set limits to the progress that may then be made, in forming virtuous habits and spreading useful information among the great body of the labouring and manufacturing population.

A very different treatment, however, is required, and with higher objects in view, for the classes of society whom birth, or fortune, or extraordinary talent, exempt from manual labor and drudgery, and who are to earn their livelihood, and improve or adorn their condition, by the feats of the head rather than by the labour of the hand. The studies of this class of youth are extended over a much longer period than those of the labouring population. Time is allowed for following out a systematic course of training, through various stages of progress, and for a series of years; and it is a training as distinct in its nature as it is different in its aim. For while nothing is to be omitted, in the longer training more than in the shorter, that tends to form virtuous habits, and inspire the love of knowledge and of nature, there is wanted, for the higher class of youth, a method comprehensive rather than compendious. It must be a course of intellectual discipline, directed, not to stock the mind with ready prepared information, but to bring out in orderly and healthful succession the several mental faculties, to give to each its appropriate nourishment and invigorating exercise, and to teach the possessor the free and dextrous use of them all; that when the time comes for sending him forth into the arduous competition and conflict of human affairs, he may be able to find a way for himself, or to make one. In this case, the point to be aimed at is not a great store of knowledge of which the mind is little better than the passive recipient. The legitimate object of the higher education, is to provide the means of evolving and perfecting the various powers and capacities of man's nature, so as to enable him, in words of Milton, 'to perform justly, skilfully, and magnanimously, all the offices, both public and private, of peace and war.'

The object of popular education, as far as the labouring classes and their children are concerned, is to create an appetite for knowledge, and a love of reading, and thus to furnish them with such harmless and improving means of mental occupation and amusement, as may save them from brutalizing pursuits, and fence them against the seduction of low and sensual indulgences.

6

Group Goals

INTRODUCTION

In the previous chapter we acknowledged the difficulty of accepting the veracity of private goals as expressed in autobiographies, but it is even more difficult to be confident that group goals faithfully express individual members' states of mind. In a sense, group goals defy validation, for there is no such thing as a "group mind." Individuals think and feel as individuals, and at times reach a measure of agreement as group members. But individuals in a group differ in the clarity with which they perceive group goals, and it is doubtful that any such goal is perceived identically by any two group members. Some may accept a group goal with eagerness because it is related to their own value systems. Others may accept it verbally because they wish to be accepted by other group members or by a particular one.

The group method (called the "project method") purports to enable a teacher to lead his pupils toward a democratic choice of a common goal, as well as toward an individual choice of a particular goal related to each one's status in the group and the role allotted to him. Some of the conventional explanations of this process, however—such as that of an individual "identifying with the group" or of the group developing a "cohesiveness" that influences wavering individuals toward a common goal acceptance—tend to oversimplify mental processes that are both complex and unique to every group member.

The illustration of a class supposedly formulating its own goals invites the suspicion of the teacher playing a significant if somewhat unobtrusive role in goal acceptance. Furthermore, without any kind of teacher direction, the goals set by the class may be reached by majority decision, again raising doubts as to how many individuals are committed to them, how many accept them merely verbally, and how many positively but tacitly reject them. What are goals for a few group members may be merely external objectives for others.

The contribution by Faunce and Bossing describes a core class supposedly setting its own goals. This selection is confronted by one of a sterner kind by Stogdill, in which the emphasis is changed from group power of manipulation to individual goal acceptance. One is reminded that individuals have value systems that are unique to each, and that each individual takes expectations of his own into the group situation. The relationships between individuals and groups are shown as complex and varied, depending partly on the relationship between individuals' value systems and those of other group members. Interaction between the individual's existing group identifications on the one hand, and his value system on the other, are considered by Stogdill to influence the acceptability of new group goals to him. And individuals differ, in any case, in the readiness with which they accept others' leadership, including others' initiation of ideas leading to goals. This selection is a salutary answer to all those who profess to find in group or class goals a strong element of personal choice as a necessary condition for group membership. While there is a need to recognize the probability of *some* clearly perceived goals within group contexts, there is a need to assert also the probability, on empirical evidence, of perceptible differences in individual-group relations and in individual group-goal appropriations.

In brief, short of empirical testing of individual attitudes, there is reason to believe that generalizations about student groups reaching group goals by democratic procedures deserve to be treated with caution. Although statements of personal and group goals are each difficult to validate, it is the personal statement rather than the group generalization that more probably reflects experience.

Roland C. Faunce and Nelson L. Bossing: The Core Class in Action[1]

Several days are . . . spent in considering whether respect and knowledge are things that can be shared by the boys and girls and the teacher and if so, what kinds of behavior will best bring these about. Such methods as working in groups and having general class discussions in order to find out what other people are thinking about a problem are suggested. These are tried out in class and the successes as well as the problems that the pupils meet in using the techniques are discussed. The conclusion is reached that shared respect and knowledge are as possible as shared power in a classroom if a real effort is made to achieve them.

They decide further that even a small group has certain rights, and certain corresponding responsibilities, if they hope to form a democratic planning group. Following is a typical list of such "rights and responsibilities," drafted by a ninth-grade class:

Rights

1. To express our own opinions
2. To help make the rules
3. To help decide the goals of the group
4. To have a free vote
5. To question the opinions of others
6. To help decide what activities are to be carried on by us

Responsibilities

1. To abide by the rules made by the group
2. To accept responsibilities laid on us by the group
3. To take an active part in the work of the group
4. To work for the welfare of the group
5. To act in such a way as to be an asset to the group.

Organizing for Problem-Attack

The next step is class organization in terms of election of class officers and writing a class constitution. It usually becomes clear early in the process of writing a constitution that it is necessary to establish the goals of the class. When this need is recognized, the class is divided into random groups, each group being responsible for preparing a list of goals. These items are then written on the board and a general discus-

[1] From Roland C. Faunce and Nelson L. Bossing, *Developing the Core Curriculum.* Englewood Cliffs, New Jersey: Prentice-Hall, Inc., 2nd edition, 1958, pp. 140-141. Reprinted by permission of Prentice-Hall, Inc.

sion follows, in the course of which the class decides on those it feels should be retained on the final list. A sample ninth grade list follows:

Class Goals

1. Gain knowledge in topic selected
2. Do research well:
   a. Use all materials possible
   b. Take good notes
3. Be able to communicate through good writing
4. Be an active and worthwhile member of a working group:
   a. Participate in all discussions
   b. Present helpful ideas as often as possible
   c. Give full attention at all times
5. Get along well with classmates
6. Express thoughts freely and well
7. Improve ability to decide things for ourselves on basis of reliable information
8. Respect another's wishes and opinions
9. Develop self-reliance
10. Increase self-confidence
11. Listen to a discussion with an open mind
12. Develop self-control

Selecting the next unit.   When the constitution is complete and the officers have been elected, a class is ready to approach the problem of selecting an area for study.

Ralph M. Stogdill: Expectation and Group Purpose[1]

Definitions[2]—*Expectation, defined as readiness for reinforcement, is a function of drive, the estimated probability of occurrence of a possible outcome, and the estimated desirability of the outcome.*

By *reinforcement* is meant the experiencing of an outcome which tends to meet, fulfill, satisfy, or confirm an expectation.

By *readiness for reinforcement* is meant the extent to which an individual is prepared or unprepared to experience, or reconciled or unreconciled to the prospect of experiencing, a possible outcome.

By *drive* is meant the level of tension and reactivity exhibited by an organism.

[1] From Ralph M. Stogdill, *Individual Behavior and Group Achievement.* New York: Oxford University Press, 1959, pp. 63, 72, 73-77, with omissions. Reprinted by permission of Oxford University Press.

[2] The subsequent discussion is partly dependent on these technical expressions (Editor's note).

The *estimated probability of occurrence of an outcome* refers to an individual's prediction, judgment, or guess relative to the likelihood that a given event will occur.

By the *estimated desirability of an outcome* is meant an individual's judgment relative to the satisfyingness of, need for, demand for, appropriateness of, or pleasantness or unpleasantness of, a possible outcome.

According to the definitions given above, estimates of probability and estimates of desirability are not opposite ends of the same continuum, and desirability is not to be regarded as a mere modifier of probability estimates. Rather, estimates of probability and estimates of desirability interact to determine the level of expectation. The operation of probability estimates is inferred if the individual is observed to exhibit a persistent postural or behavioral orientation toward, and a preparatory readiness for experiencing, an outcome. The operation of desirability estimates is inferred if the individual is observed to exhibit satisfaction or disappointment with an outcome for which he was prepared. An individual tends either to accept or reject an outcome for which no prior preparation was possible.

*   *   *   *

Individuals tend to formulate judgments in terms of scales of estimate that appear to be related not only to the objective situation but also to their past experiences. Thus, an individual's perception of a situation is determined both by the information that he derives from the situation and by the set or expectation in terms of which he views the situation. The desirability of a situation is estimated in reference to internalized scales and norms of value which are determined by past experience. That which conforms to these norms tends to be most readily perceived, and that which departs from the norms tends to be rejected.

Since the strong reinforcement of expectation tends not only to confirm desirability estimates but also to strengthen other related expectations that are highly valued, the individual develops systems of more or less highly interrelated value expectations relative to his family, school, community, church, political party, nation, work group, and so on. These different systems may be mutually reinforcing or they may be in conflict with each other. Young people frequently experience conflict between the values acquired from their parents and those acquired from their age peers. They may also perceive conflict between the values acquired at church and those acquired from their science teachers.

A personal *value system* may be defined as a highly generalized set of expectations in which desirability estimates are mutually confirmed with little reference to probability estimates, and which serves as a referent or criterion for evaluating the desirability of alternative outcomes. The degree of generalization among these value systems may be conceived as so great that they are reinforced by almost all relevant outcomes. Since they are reinforced by satisfying as well as unsatisfying outcomes, and are little diminished by the failure of outcomes to confirm their validity, they are very resistant to modification and are essentially non-extinguishable. Because of their high degree of independence of validating outcomes, they come to serve as stable reference points in terms of which experienced outcomes are evaluated as satisfying or unsatisfying. They also serve as comparing criteria and, as such, enable the individual to evaluate the values of other persons, groups, and subgroups. The prejudiced person is one who makes evaluations in terms of his value systems without reference to the objective validity of his judgments.

According to Tolman,[1] experience tends either to confirm or disconfirm expectations. It is here proposed that the *validity* of an expectation is determined by the confirmation of probability estimates. A rational expectation is one that is formulated in terms of the estimated probability of outcomes. The estimate need not be accurate in order to be rational, but the criterion of its validity is the occurrence or nonoccurrence of the predicted outcomes. Validation is the confirming reinforcement of a rational expectation.

Experienced outcomes which reinforce, or correspond with, a desirability estimate confirm the *value* of an expectation. It is proposed that desirability estimates are highly reinforceable by related expectations and may exhibit very little decrement despite the lack of reinforcement of probability estimates. However, the value of an expectation may be diminished by an outcome which confirms probability estimates but fails to confirm desirability estimates.

Outcomes may confirm estimates of probability but not of desirability; or they may confirm estimates of desirability but not of probability. Either set of outcomes may prove unsatisfying. More important is the fact that it is only when desirability estimates and probability estimates are reinforced simultaneously that value systems are subjected to reality testing. A highly valued outcome may not prove to be a validating outcome if the individual entertains little or no expectation of its occurrence, is uncertain, misestimates the probability of its occurrence, or experiences the outcome under such inconsistent and discrepant circumstances that no rational prediction is possible. Thus, although an out-

[1] Tolman, E. C., *Purposive Behavior in Animals and Men*. New York: Appleton-Century, 1932.

come may prove to be highly valued, it may provide no valid basis for estimating the probability of its occurrence in the future.

That values are reinforced by satisfying as well as unsatisfying outcomes is evidenced in political beliefs. If the political party of one's choice is in power, good times are attributed to the wise action of the politicians, while bad times are explained by the force of circumstances. When the opposing party is in power, good times are attributed to the rising trend of events, and bad times to stupid politics. Strongly reinforced value systems appear to be affected very little by reality testing.

The integrity of the individual is founded on the consistency of his value systems. A member may withdraw his vote from the party of his choice or may withdraw his membership from a group if he perceives it as being no longer capable of acting in accord with his personal values. These values need not be personally oriented. They may be concerned with the welfare of family, friends, nation, or humanity at large. They may refer to the welfare of various groups to which the individual belongs. But, no matter what their objective reference, they can be traced back to the individual. Whatever happens to family, friends, and membership groups has an impact on the individual. It is due to the fact that he exhibits a preference for certain outcomes (for self and others) that his generalized expectation systems may be called value systems.

Individuals differ in what they value. The same objectively observable outcomes are not responded to alike by all persons. When alternative outcomes are available, a more highly valued reward tends to exert a stronger reinforcing effect than does a reward of lesser perceived value. However, the effect of a reward in a series of reinforcements is determined not by its absolute magnitude, but by the range of magnitudes perceived to be available. In order to estimate the satisfyingness of an outcome to an individual, it is necessary to know the frame of reference in terms of which his expectations have been formulated.

Individual Values and Group Affiliation

The individual is thrust at birth into a social situation. Both the quality of nurturance and the schedule of care which he receives in infancy may establish expectations relative to the good will and dependability of other persons that last through adult life. Since initial reinforcements exert stronger effects than later reinforcements, and since strongly reinforced desirability estimates appear to be resistant to extinction, it seems reasonable to accept as valid the conclusions of numerous clinical observers who report that enduring patterns of behavior and belief are fixed early in childhood. Many of the child's expectations are set by the training and treatment he receives in the home. Other expectations are acquired in the classroom, in the playground, and in other social situations. The expectations acquired in one group may be exhibited by the individual in other groups.

It seems unnecessary to postulate any biologically determined drive or need for group affiliation or social co-operation. Any patterns of social behavior which suggest the possible operation of such factors can be more simply explained in terms of learning and reinforcement of expectation. As soon as habitable frontiers become accessible to human exploitation they are sought by individuals who exhibit little evidence of drive for affiliation or cooperation. Many individuals who are compelled by necessity to participate in group life exhibit only a marginal degree of membership. The clinician encounters numerous clients who have experienced such inconsistent and painful reinforcement of expectation that they not only mistrust all affiliative interaction but feel no secure sense of personal identity.

An individual's sense of personal identity and his identification of himself with other persons and groups seems best understood in the light of his history of social reinforcements. He tends to identify himself in some degree, either positively or negatively, with those individuals and groups that have been influential in shaping his expectations. According to Newcomb,[1] any group with which an individual identifies or compares himself, either positively or negatively, may be regarded as a reference group. The individual evaluates possible outcomes not only in terms of his value systems but also in terms of the perceived values and experiences of his reference groups. An individual may or may not be a member of one or more of his reference groups.

When individuals are free to choose, they appear to seek the companionship of persons whose values are similar to their own and to join groups whose goals and activities tend to reinforce their own value systems. It seems probable that the individual will continue to identify himself with a membership group that initiates a strongly reinforced expectation and continues to reinforce it. However, if reinforcement of a highly valued expectation is discontinued, the individual may either reject the group or experience a conflict of loyalties in relation to it. A group that arouses a strong negative or unpleasant expectation may be rejected.

The willingness of a member to permit a group to structure his expectations is likely to be determined by the extent to which he perceives the goals of the group and the value systems of its members to be in accord with his own value systems and those of the reference groups with

[1] Newcomb, T.M., *Personality and Social Change.* New York: Dryden Press, 1943.

which he most strongly identifies himself. Thus, some individuals appear to identify themselves quickly with a new group, while others never seem to accept the group or identify themselves with it. Individuals not only differ in their value systems and reference group identifications, but they also appear to differ in the extent to which they are willing to accept structure that is initiated and controlled by other persons. The individual is likely to accept, or even to demand, structure in a new group if he perceives a stable system of goals, norms, and related expectations to reinforce his own value systems and to increase the probability of experiencing satisfying outcomes. However, the individual who expects to experience negatively valued outcomes and who perceives the goals of the group to be in conflict with his own value systems may oppose the group structure even though he accepts membership in it and conforms sufficiently to retain his membership. Thus, an individual's performance in a group may be determined not only by those expectations that are structured by the group but also by the expectations that he brings into the group. However, some persons may enter the group because they perceive no more satisfying alternatives to be available or because they seek to avoid certain unpleasant consequences attendant upon avoiding membership in the group. They may participate voluntarily even though they find the experience unpleasant or disapprove of the activities of the group. It is apparent that membership in a group is not necessarily dependent upon a correspondence between individual values and group purpose. It seems probable that value systems and reference group identifications interact to determine to a large extent an individual's acceptance or rejection of the goals and structures of the groups to which he belongs.

IV

The nature of aims
in education

7

Theoretical Approaches to Aims

INTRODUCTION

Parts I, II, and III are related in so far as they all deal with aims of education that have been adopted, either as plans for others or as plans for the self. Part IV is distinct from each of these in that it is concerned with theorizing about the *nature* of aims of education, or about aims of education per se.

What is the relation between the theory of aims and the formulation of aims? One may consider theory and practice in this sense at two distinct levels. First, at a very general level, one may consider the actual *formulation* of aims of education (F), which are intended to influence educational practice (P) in curriculum making, classroom teaching, and so forth. Second, at a more analytical level, one may consider a *theory* of aims (T), which is intended as a guide to the formulation of aims. If T is justified, it should clearly precede F; that is, if it performs a role of clarification a case might be made for it as a discipline in its own right—a discipline requiring close examination before the task of actually propounding aims of education begins. It could never be defended that agreement on the fundamental principles of a theory of aims, including principles of procedure to guide the formulation of an aim, would lead to unanimity in the actual formulation. Rather it would be, first, that a grasp of theory might lead at a practical or experiential level, to an understanding of what an educator is attempting when he formulates aims for others (his general relationship to the student, what his opportunities for influencing others might be, what his right to influence might be, and so forth). Second, a grasp of theory might lead, at an abstract level, to an understanding of the logic of formulating aims (involving perhaps a consideration of suggested rules for aim-making, such as a development of argument from openly stated premises, and the relationship between belief and practice). Assuming then that a theory has been developed with proper concern for both logic and experience, and that its statement is intelligible and acceptable to practicing educators, one might expect a minimum of confusion in an educator's progression from theory to formulation to practice. The particular function of theory would be to discipline those who formulate aims, so they may be prevented, as far as possible, from misleading practicing educators in either plans or practices. The theoretical advantages ensuing would perhaps be roughly proportional to the conflict and confusion observed in current aim statements.

It may be argued, of course, that every formulation of an aim implies a theory of aims, that it is not possible to be consistent in expressing aims without at the same time conveying some of the principles on which they rest. By keeping the illustrations of Parts I–III in mind, one may be able to infer something of their authors' unstated views on what properly constitutes an effective aim of education. It would be implied theory, for instance, to discover that principles of logic have in fact been followed by aim statements that are unambiguous, or that are clearly deducible from initial premises. On the other hand, from some instances of formulation it may be reasonable to infer an absence of theory, or a need for more rigor and clarity in theory. The abstraction and attenuation of supposedly implicit aims are, however, frequently suspect. If one were to indulge in dilettante theorizing, for instance, on what is "implied" in Parts I–III, one might read off something of a theory of aims of education from the fundamental distinction between them: either that aims are to be propounded for youth by experienced and knowledgeable adults, or that they are in all cases to be the personal choices of youth.

In this chapter, Dewey, Peters, and Gotesky each analyze the nature of aims in education, though in a complementary rather than in an antithetical fashion. Dewey is partly concerned with inferring the nature of aims from experience and partly with making rules for aims; he is interested in aims generally and educational aims specifically. Peters challenges the *need* for educators to have aims, although he recognizes the advantages that accrue from them. Gotesky is interested primarily in analyzing kinds of aims and showing relationships among them. Common to the three—although varying in degree from one to another—are an awareness of the need to clarify the language of aims, and an exclusive concentration of interest in the empirical world. Of the three, Dewey is the most distinctively empirical, not merely in his reliance on observation within the world of experience, but also in the experimental orientation of his thought. Both Peters and Gotesky are strongly influenced by Dewey, who provides for each the initial cue for inquiry. Dewey and Gotesky are related in their common awareness of the flexibility of aims.

Dewey's viewpoint is conveyed in selections from *Democracy and Education* and *Theory of Valuation*. The key words to an understanding of Dewey's theory of aims are *observation, experience,* and *intelligence.* First, by observation of people in the act of aiming, Dewey infers that there is no hard and fast separation of ends and means. A means is an end until the end based on it is achieved; that end then becomes a means to another end in the future. Ends and means have no permanent status. Second, aims belong to an observable world of experience. There is nothing that can be called "the ultimate aim of education." The popular distinction between "immediate" and "ultimate" in aim-statements is as misleading as that between ends and means. The only intelligible meaning to be given to an "immediate aim" is that it is the first one arising from a desire. The only intelligible meaning to be given to an "ultimate aim" is that it is the last desire a person has in a particular situation. It is neither fixed nor final. There is no such thing in experience as an end-in-itself. Aims are as fluid as the stream of experience to which they belong; experience is free-flowing, continuous, and capable of constant adaptation to meet the needs of situations as they arise. Third, intelligence combines with observation to keep the focus on experience. Intelligence comes into play in attempting to resolve a temporary obstruction to the fulfilment of one's desires. Indeed, desires arise only when something is the matter. The method of intelligence is to set up ends and means as a unified plan for each particular situation. If ends and means are not planned in conjunction absurdities arise, as Charles Lamb demonstrates in his essay on roast pork.

Dewey's most significant conclusion from this triple emphasis on observation, experience, and intelligence is that education is its own end. Nothing lies beyond education to which education can be said to aim;

there is nothing intelligible *beyond* education, nothing intelligible beyond life experience. The territory of the extrinsic merely baffles intelligence.

In Peters' contribution the extrinsic is again the *bête noire*. The method of attack is to apply *observation* and *analysis* to *experience*. Observation of aims without experience shows him that "omnibus ends" such as "self-realization" are never encountered among individuals pursuing ends. They exist only as "premeditations"—remote ideals in the minds of aim-makers. The expression in high-sounding generalities misleads. There are, in fact, no educational means that can be regarded as instrumental to achieving such supposed ends. Indeed, they are not strictly aims or ends at all, for they merely express their authors' preferences for doing certain things in certain ways. Unlike Dewey who prefers to see educational experience always in motion, Peters concentrates on a single isolated segment of activity. "We can see what values educators are holding," he seems to say, "by the way they are going about things. We don't have to look ahead toward the end of the process to see what they're aiming at—they may in fact have no end in mind!" If an educator's stated ends are extrinsic and pompous, their very irrelevance to actual experience can thus be demonstrated, Peters argues, by freezing a portion of experience and discovering in it, as it is examined, that the educator is asserting his values *through* the principles of procedure he supports. Thus, he may prefer drill methods of teaching because of his value of authority. He may have no such end-in-view as character building, or development of dispositions of self-discipline. Or, if he expresses an omnibus end such as the self-realization of his pupils, that may be a remote ideal or an inert concept in his own mind unrelated to his educational activities.

Peter's aversion to vagueness and vacuity is brought to a head in his demand that the "brass-tacks" type of question be asked about any aim: "What procedures are to be adopted in order to implement it?" The extrinsic aim is only a pseudo-aim. All aims worthy of the name are connected with experience. It is these that he supports in the second selection, acknowledging that aim-making is a way of clarifying what the educator is trying to do.

Whereas Peters takes a short-range view of the educational aim-maker at work, Gotesky emphasizes *analysis* and *classification*. In his examination of words for meaning, and in his analytical bent, he is akin to Peters in this sense. His impulse, though, is more constructive. By classification he attempts to clarify the various kinds of aim-words commonly used in education. Peters takes a closer view of aims in experience than Dewey, but Gotesky focuses at still shorter range, the object of his observations being a group of aim-words rather than a segment of experience.

Gotesky's classification can best be grasped by relating his distinctions to those outlined in the General Introduction. First, his *objective* approximates the specific, simple objectives illustrated in Chapter 3. Second, his goal is closest to, but not identical with, the attitudinal disposition of the type described as complex in Chapter 4, where it is only sometimes compounded of identifiable, separate objectives. However, "goal," as illustrated in Chapter 5, is characterized as uniquely *personal*, applying to both ideals (unattainable) and objectives (attainable). Third, Gotesky's use of "ideal" as a cluster of goals expressing a common purpose of goals and objectives is distinct from the concept of ideal as illustrated in the first chapter, for Gotesky's ideal *is* attainable. Fourth, the classification of aims of education proposed in the General Introduction makes no provision for anything corresponding to Gotesky's "the-ideals," with their formation of generalized ideals into coherent structures. This concept has some affinity with particular personality theories, but one may feel some uneasiness in accepting it in principle as an educational end-in-view.

Gotesky's common ground with Dewey is his logical-empirical inclination. He admits that the relations among his ends-in-view are very complex, with continuous interactions among them. Objectives can modify goals or ideals, or reject them; goals can give rise to new ideals or objectives, or reject the old; ideals can give rise to new goals, or similarly reject the old. While logic is the tool, the material for his classification is drawn from the natural world.

Indeed, the selections represented in this chapter have common ground in their rejection of normative ends viewed as extrinsic to education itself. Viewpoints on the nature of educational aims which do not share the common naturalistic bias of these selections will be reviewed in the concluding chapter.

John Dewey: Aims in Education[1]

In our search for aims in education, we are not concerned with finding an end outside of the educative process to which education is subordinate. Our whole conception forbids. We are rather concerned with the contrast which exists when aims belong within the process in which they operate and when they are set up from without. And the latter state of affairs must obtain when social relationships are not equitably balanced. For in that case, some portions of the whole social group will find their aims determined by an external dictation; their aims will not arise from the free growth of their own experience, and their nominal aims will be means to more ulterior ends of others rather than truly their own.

Our first question is to define the nature of an aim so far as it falls within an activity, instead of being furnished from without. We approach the definition by a contrast of mere *results* with *ends*. Any exhibition of energy has results. The wind blows about the sands of the desert; the position of the grains is changed. Here is a result, an effect, but not an *end*. For there is nothing in the outcome which completes or fulfills what went before it. There is mere spatial redistribution. One state of affairs is just as good as any other. Consequently there is no basis upon which to select an earlier state of affairs as a beginning, a later as an end, and to consider what intervenes as a process of transformation and realization.

Consider for example the activities of bees in contrast with the changes in the sands when the wind blows them about. The results of the bees' actions may be called ends not because they are designed or consciously intended, but because they are true terminations or completions of what has preceded. When the bees gather pollen and make wax and build cells, each step prepares the way for the next. When cells are built, the queen lays eggs in them; when eggs are laid, they are sealed and bees brood them and keep them at a temperature required to hatch them. When they are hatched, bees feed the young till they can take care of themselves. Now we are so familiar with such facts, that we are apt to dismiss them on the ground that life and instinct are a kind of miraculous thing anyway. Thus we fail to note what the essential characteristic of the event is; namely, the significance of the temporal place and order of each element; the way each prior event leads into its successor while the

[1] From John Dewey, *Democracy and Education*. New York: Free Press of Glencoe, paperback edition, 1966, pp. 100-110, with omissions. Reprinted by permission of The Macmillan Company, copyright 1916 by The Macmillan Company; renewed 1944 by John Dewey.

successor takes up what is furnished and utilizes it for some other stage, until we arrive at the end, which, as it were, summarizes and finishes off the process.

Since aims relate always to results, the first thing to look to when it is a question of aims, is whether the work assigned possesses intrinsic continuity. Or is it a mere serial aggregate of acts, first doing one thing and then another? To talk about an educational aim when approximately each act of a pupil is dictated by the teacher, when the only order in the sequence of his acts is that which comes from the assignment of lessons and the giving of directions by another, is to talk nonsense. It is equally fatal to an aim to permit capricious or discontinuous action in the name of spontaneous self-expression. An aim implies an orderly and ordered activity, one in which the order consists in the progressive completing of a process. Given an activity having a time span and cumulative growth within the time succession, an aim means foresight in advance of the end or possible termination. If bees anticipated the consequences of their activity, if they perceived their end in imaginative foresight, they would have the primary element in an aim. Hence it is nonsense to talk about the aim of education—or any other undertaking—where conditions do not permit of foresight of results, and do not stimulate a person to look ahead to see what the outcome of a given activity is to be.

In the next place the aim as a foreseen end gives direction to the activity, it is not an idle view of a mere spectator, but influences the steps taken to reach the end. The foresight functions in three ways. In the first place, it involves careful observation of the given conditions to see what are the means available for reaching the end, and to discover the hindrances in the way. In the second place, it suggests the proper order or sequence in the use of means. It facilitates an economical selection and arrangement. In the third place, it makes choice of alternatives possible. If we can predict the outcome of acting this way or that, we can then compare the value of the two courses of action; we can pass judgment upon their relative desirability. If we know that stagnant water breeds mosquitoes and that they are likely to carry disease, we can, disliking that anticipated result, take steps to avert it. Since we do not anticipate results as intellectual onlookers, but as persons concerned in the outcome, we are partakers in the process which produces the result. We intervene to bring about this result or that.

Of course these three points are closely connected with one another. We can definitely foresee results only as we make careful scrutiny of present conditions, and the importance of the outcome supplies the motive for observations. The more adequate our observations, the more varied is the scene of conditions and obstructions that presents itself, and the more numerous are the alternatives between which choice may be made. In turn, the more numerous the recognized possibilities of the situation, or alternatives of action, the more meaning does the chosen activity possess, and the more flexibly controllable is it. Where only a single outcome has been thought of, the mind has nothing else to think of; the meaning attaching to the act is limited. One only steams ahead toward the mark. Sometimes such a narrow course may be effective. But if unexpected difficulties offer themselves, one has not as many resources at command as if he had chosen the same line of action after a broader survey of the possibilities of the field. He cannot make needed readjustments readily.

The net conclusion is that acting with an aim is one with acting intelligently. To foresee a terminus of an act is to have a basis upon which to observe, to select, and to order objects and our own capacities. To do these things means to have a mind—for mind is precisely intentional purposeful activity controlled by perception of facts and their relationships to one another. To have a mind to do a thing is to foresee a future possibility; it is to have a plan for its accomplishment; it is to note the means which make the plan capable of execution and the obstructions in the way,—or, if it is really a *mind* to do the thing and not a vague aspiration—it is to have a plan which takes account of resources and difficulties. Mind is capacity to refer present conditions to future results, and future consequences to present conditions. And these traits are just what is meant by having an aim or a purpose. A man is stupid or blind or unintelligent—lacking in mind—just in the degree in which in any activity he does not know what he is about, namely, the probable consequences of his acts. A man is imperfectly intelligent when he contents himself with looser guesses about the outcome than is needful, just taking a chance with his luck, or when he forms plans apart from study of the actual conditions, including his own capacities. Such relative absence of mind means to make our feelings the measure of what is to happen. To be intelligent we must "stop, look, listen" in making the plan of an activity.

* * * *

The Criteria of Good Aims.   We may apply the results of our discussion to a consideration of the criteria involved in a correct establishing of aims. The aim set up must be an outgrowth of existing conditions. It must be based upon a consideration of what is already going on; upon the resources and difficulties of the situation. Theories about the proper end of our activities—educational and moral theories—often violate this principle. They assume ends lying *outside* our activities; ends foreign to the concrete makeup of the situation; ends which issue from some outside source. Then the problem is to bring our activities to bear upon the realization of these externally supplied ends. They are something for which we *ought* to act. In any case such "aims" limit intelligence; they are not the expression of mind in foresight, observation, and choice of the better among alternative possibilities. They limit intelligence because, given ready-made, they must be imposed by some authority external to intelligence, leaving to the latter nothing but a mechanical choice of means.

We have spoken as if aims could be completely formed prior to the attempt to realize them. This impression must now be qualified. The aim as it first emerges is a mere tentative sketch. The act of striving to realize it tests its worth. If it suffices to direct activity successfully, nothing more is required, since its whole function is to set a mark in advance; and at times a mere hint may suffice. But usually—at least in complicated situations—acting upon it brings to light conditions which had been overlooked. This calls for revision of the original aim; it has to be added to and subtracted from. An aim must, then, be *flexible*; it must be capable of alteration to meet circumstances. An end established externally to the process of action is always rigid. Being inserted or imposed from without, it is not supposed to have a working relationship to the concrete conditions of the situation. What happens in the course of action neither confirms, refutes, nor alters it. Such an end can only be insisted upon. The failure that results from its lack of adaptation is attributed simply to the perverseness of conditions, not to the fact that the end is not reasonable under the circumstances. The value of a legitimate aim, on the contrary, lies in the fact that we can use it to change conditions. It is a method for dealing with conditions so as to effect desirable alterations in them. . . . A good aim surveys the present state of experience of pupils, and forming a tentative plan of treatment, keeps the plan constantly in view and yet modifies it as conditions develop. The aim, in short, is experimental, and hence constantly growing as it is tested in action.

The aim must always represent a freeing of activities. The term *end in view* is suggestive, for it puts before the mind the termination or conclusion of some process. The only way in which we can define an activity is by putting before ourselves the objects in which it terminates —as one's aim in shooting is the target. But we must remember that the *object* is only a mark or sign by which the mind specifies the *activity* one desires to carry out. Strictly speaking, not the target but *hitting* the target is the end in view; one *takes* aim by means of the target, but also by the sight on the gun. The different objects which are thought of are means of *directing* the activity. . . .

In contrast with fulfilling some process in order that activity may go on, stands the static character of an end which is imposed from without the activity. It is always conceived of as fixed; it is *something* to be attained and possessed. When one has such a notion, activity is a mere unavoidable means to something else; it is not significant or important on its own account. As compared with the end it is but a necessary evil; something which must be gone through before one can reach the object which is alone worth while. In other words, the external idea of the aim leads to a separation of means from end, while an end which grows up within an activity as plan for its direction is always both ends and means, the distinction being only one of convenience. Every means is a temporary end until we have attained it. Every end becomes a means of carrying activity further as soon as it is achieved. We call it end when it marks off the future direction of the activity in which we are engaged; means when it marks off the present direction. Every divorce of end from means diminishes by that much the significance of the activity and tends to reduce it to a drudgery from which one would escape if he could....

Applications in Education.   There is nothing peculiar about educational aims.... Aims mean acceptance of responsibility for the observations, anticipations, and arrangements required in carrying on a function —whether farming or educating. Any aim is of value so far as it assists observation, choice, and planning in carrying on activity from moment to moment and hour to hour; if it gets in the way of the individual's own common sense (as it will surely do if imposed from without or accepted on authority) it does harm.

And it is well to remind ourselves that education as such has no aims. Only persons, parents, and teachers, etc., have aims, not an abstract idea like education. And consequently their purposes are indefinitely varied, differing with different children, changing as children grow and with the growth of experience on the part of the one who teaches. Even the most valid aims which can be put in words will, as words, do more harm than good unless one recognizes that they are not aims, but rather suggestions to educators as to how to observe, how to look ahead, and how to choose in liberating and directing the energies of the concrete situations in which they find themselves....

Bearing these qualifications in mind, we shall proceed to state some of the characteristics found in all good educational aims. An educational aim must be founded upon the intrinsic activities and needs (including original instincts and acquired habits) of the given individual to be educated. The tendency of such an aim as preparation is, as we have seen, to omit existing powers, and find the aim in some remote accomplishment or responsibility. In general, there is a disposition to take considerations which are dear to the hearts of adults and set them up as ends irrespective of the capacities of those educated. There is also an inclination to propound aims which are so uniform as to neglect the specific powers and requirements of an individual, forgetting that all learning is something which happens to an individual at a given time and place. ... But it is one thing to use adult accomplishments as a context in which to place and survey the doings of childhood and youth; it is quite another to set them up as a fixed aim without regard to the concrete activities of those educated.

An aim must be capable of translation into a method of coöperating with the activities of those undergoing instruction. It must suggest the kind of environment needed to liberate and to organize *their* capacities. Unless it lends itself to the construction of specific procedures, and unless these procedures test, correct, and amplify the aim, the latter is worthless....

The vice of externally imposed ends has deep roots. Teachers receive them from superior authorities; these authorities accept them from what is current in the community. The teachers impose them upon children. As a first consequence, the intelligence of the teacher is not free; it is confined to receiving the aims laid down from above. Too rarely is the individual teacher so free from the dictation of authoritative supervisor, textbook on methods, prescribed course of study, etc., that he can let his mind come to close quarters with the pupil's mind and the subject matter. This distrust of the teacher's experience is then reflected in lack of confidence in the responses of pupils. The latter receive their aims through a double or treble external imposition, and are constantly confused by the conflict between the aims which are natural to their own experience at the time and those in which they are taught to acquiesce. Until the democratic criterion of the intrinsic significance of every growing experience is recognized, we shall be intellectually confused by the demand for adaptation to external aims.

Educators have to be on their guard against ends that are alleged to be general and ultimate. Every activity, however specific, is, of course, general in its ramified connections, for it leads out indefinitely into other things. So far as a general idea makes us more alive to these connections, it cannot be too general. But "general" also means "abstract," or detached from all specific context. And such abstractness means remoteness, and throws us back, once more, upon teaching and learning as mere means of getting ready for an end disconnected from the means. That education is literally and all the time its own reward means that no alleged study or discipline is educative unless it is worth while in its own immediate having. A truly general aim broadens the outlook; it stimulates one to take more consequences (connections) into account. . . .

* * * * *

Summary.   An aim denotes the result of any natural process brought to consciousness and made a factor in determining present observation and choice of ways of acting. It signifies that an activity has become intelligent. Specifically it means foresight of the alternative consequences attendant upon acting in a given situation in different ways, and the use of what is anticipated to direct observation and experiment. A true aim is thus opposed at every point to an aim which is imposed upon a process of action from without. The latter is fixed and rigid; it is not a stimulus to intelligence in the given situation, but is an externally dictated order to do such and such things. Instead of connecting directly with present activities, it is remote, divorced from the means by which it is to be reached. Instead of suggesting a freer and better balanced activity, it is a limit set to activity. In education, the currency of these externally imposed aims is responsible for the emphasis put upon the notion of preparation for a remote future and for rendering the work of both teacher and pupil mechanical and slavish.

John Dewey: Ends and Values *and* The Continuum of Ends-Means[1]

It has been remarked more than once that the source of the trouble with theories which relate value to desire and interest, and then proceed to make a sharp division between prizing and appraisal, between ends and means, is the failure to make an empirical investigation of the actual conditions under which desires and interest arise and function, and in which end-objects, ends-in-view, acquire their actual contents. Such an analysis will now be undertaken.

When we inquire into the actual emergence of desire and its object and the value-property ascribed to the latter (instead of merely manipulating dialectically the general concept of desire), it is as plain as anything can be that desires arise only when "there is something the matter," when there is some "trouble" in an existing situation. When analyzed, this "something the matter" is found to spring from the fact that there is something lacking, wanting, in the existing situation as it stands, an absence which produces conflict in the elements that do exist. When

[1] From John Dewey, *Theory of Valuation.* Chicago: The University of Chicago Press, International Encyclopedia of Unified Science, 1939, vol. II, no. 4, pp. 33-35, 40-46, with omissions. Reprinted by permission of the University of Chicago Press.

things are going completely smoothly, desires do not arise, and there is no occasion to project ends-in-view, for "going smoothly" signifies that there is no need for effort and struggle. It suffices to let things take their "natural" course. There is no occasion to investigate what it would be better to have happen in the future, and hence no projection of an end-object.

Now vital impulses and acquired habits often operate without the intervention of an end-in-view or a purpose. . . . But if and when *desire* and *an end-in-view* intervene between the occurrence of a vital impulse or a habitual tendency and the execution of an activity, then the impulse or tendency is to some degree modified and transformed: a statement which is purely tautological, since the occurrence of a desire related to an end-in-view *is* a transformation of a prior impulse or routine habit. It is only in such cases that valuation occurs. This fact . . . is of much greater importance than it might at first sight seem to be in connection with the theory which relates valuation to desire and interest, for it proves that valuation takes place only when there is something the matter; when there is some trouble to be done away with, some need, lack, or privation to be made good, some conflict of tendencies to be resolved by means of changing existing conditions. This fact in turn proves that there is present an intellectual factor—a factor of inquiry—whenever there is valuation, for the end-in-view is formed and projected as that which, if acted upon, will supply the existing need or lack and resolve the existing conflict. It follows from this that the difference in different desires and their correlative ends-in-view depends upon two things. The first is the adequacy with which inquiry into the lacks and conflicts of the existing situation has been carried on. The second is the adequacy of the inquiry into the likelihood that the particular end-in-view which is set up will, if acted upon, actually fill the existing need, satisfy the requirements constituted by what is needed, and do away with conflict by directing activity so as to institute a unified state of affairs. . . . Things can be anticipated or foreseen *as ends* or outcomes only in terms of the conditions by which they are brought into existence. It is simply impossible to have an end-in-view or to anticipate the consequences of any proposed line of action save upon the basis of some, however slight, consideration of the means by which it can be brought into existence. Otherwise, there is no genuine desire but an idle fantasy, a futile wish. That vital impulses and acquired habits are capable of expending themselves in the channels of daydreaming and building castles in the air is unfortunately true. But by description the contents of dreams and air castles are *not* ends-in-view, and what makes them fantasies is precisely the fact that they are *not* formed in terms of actual conditions serving as means of their actualization. *Propositions in which things (acts and materials) are appraised as means enter necessarily into desires and interests that determine end-values.* Hence the importance of the inquiries that result in the appraisal of things as means.

Those who have read and enjoyed Charles Lamb's essay on the origin of roast pork have probably not been conscious that their enjoyment of its absurdity was due to perception of the absurdity of any "end" which is set up apart from the means by which it is to be attained and apart from its own further functions as means. Nor is it probable that Lamb himself wrote the story as deliberate travesty of the theories that make such a separation. Nonetheless, that is the whole point of the tale. The story, it will be remembered, is that roast pork was first enjoyed when a house in which pigs were confined was accidentally burned down. While searching in the ruins, the owners touched the pigs that had been roasted in the fire and scorched their fingers. Impulsively bringing their fingers to their mouths to cool them, they experienced a new taste. Enjoying the taste, they henceforth set themselves to building houses, inclosing pigs in them, and then burning the houses down. Now, if ends-in-view are what they are entirely apart from means, and have their value independently of valuation of means, there is nothing absurd, nothing ridiculous, in this procedure, for the end attained, the *de facto* termination, *was* eating and enjoying roast pork, and that was just the end desired. Only when the end attained is estimated in terms of the means employed—the building and burning-down of houses in comparison with other available means by which the desired result in view might be attained—is there anything absurd or unreasonable about the method employed.

The story has a direct bearing upon another point, the meaning of "intrinsic." *Enjoyment* of the taste of roast pork may be said to be immediate, although even so the enjoyment would be a somewhat troubled one, for those who have memory, by the thought of the needless cost at which it was obtained. But to pass from immediacy of enjoyment to something called "intrinsic value" is a leap for which there is no ground. The *value* of enjoyment of an object *as* an attained end is a value of something which is being an end, an outcome, stands in relation to the means of which it is the consequence. Hence if the object in question is prized *as* an end or "final" value, it is valued *in this relation* or as mediated. The first time roast pork was enjoyed, it was *not* an end-value, since by description it was not the result of desire, foresight, and intent. Upon subsequent occasions it was, by description, the outcome of prior foresight, desire, and effort, and hence occupied the position of an end-in-view. There are occasions in which previous effort enhances enjoyment of what is attained. But there are also many occasions in which persons find that, when they have attained something as an end, they have paid too high a price in effort and in sacrifice of other ends. In such situations *enjoyment* of the end attained is itself *valued,* for it is not taken in its immediacy but in terms of its cost—a fact fatal to its being regarded as "an end-in-itself," a self-contradictory term in any case.

The story throws a flood of light upon what is usually meant by the maxim "the end justifies the means" and also upon the popular objection to it. Applied in this case, it would mean that the value of the attained end, the eating of roast pork, was such as to warrant the price paid in the means by which it was attained—destruction of dwelling-houses and sacrifice of the values to which they contribute. The conception involved in the maxim that "the end justifies the means" is basically the same as that in the notion of ends-in-themselves; indeed, from a historical point of view, it is the fruit of the latter, for only the conception that certain things are ends-in-themselves can warrant the belief that the relation of ends-means is unilateral, proceeding exclusively from end to means. When the maxim is compared with empirically ascertained facts, it is equivalent to holding one of two views, both of which are incompatible with the facts. One of the views is that only the specially selected "end" held in view will actually be brought into existence by the means used, something miraculously intervening to prevent the means employed from having their other usual effects; the other (and more probable) view is that, as compared with the importance of the selected and uniquely prized end, other consequences may be completely ignored and brushed aside no matter how intrinsically obnoxious they are. This arbitrary selection of some one part of the attained consequences as *the* end and hence as the warrant of means used (no matter how objectionable are their *other* consequences) is the fruit of holding that *it,* as *the* end, is an end-in-itself, and hence possessed of "value" irrespective of all its existential relations. And this notion is inherent in *every* view that assumes that "ends" can be valued apart from appraisal of the things used as means in attaining them. The sole alternative to the view that *the* end is an arbitrarily selected part of actual consequences which *as* "the end" then justifies the use of means irrespective of the other consequences they produce, is that desires, ends-in-view, and consequences achieved be valued in turn as means of further consequences. . . .

We are thus brought back to a point already set forth. In all the physical sciences (using "physical" here as a synonym for *nonhuman*) it is now taken for granted that all "effects" are also "causes," or, stated more accurately, that nothing happens which is *final* in the sense that it is not part of an ongoing stream of events. If this principle, with the accompanying discrediting of belief in objects that are ends but not means, is employed in dealing with distinctive human phenomena, it necessarily follows that the distinction between ends and means is temporal and relational. Every condition that has to be brought into existence in order to serve as means is, *in that connection,* an object of desire and an end-in-view, while the end actually reached is a means to future ends as well as a test of valuations previously made. . . .

*   *   *   *

A value is *final* in the sense that it represents the conclusion of a process of analytic appraisals of conditions operating in a concrete case, the conditions including impulses and desires on one side and external conditions on the other. Any conclusion reached by an inquiry that is taken to warrant the conclusion is "final" for that case. "Final" here has logical force. The quality or property of value that is correlated with the *last* desire formed in the process of valuation is, tautologically, ultimate for that particular situation. It applies, however, to a specifiable temporal *means-end relation* and not to something which is an end per se. There is a fundamental difference between a final property or quality and the property or quality of finality.

R. S. Peters: Must An Educator Have An Aim?[1]

Given that 'education' implies, first, some commendable state of mind and, secondly, some experience that is thought to lead up to or to contribute to it, and given also that people are usually deliberately put in the way of such experiences, it is only too easy to think of the whole business in terms of models like that of building a bridge or going on a journey. The commendable state of mind is thought of as an end to be aimed at, and the experiences which lead up to it are regarded as means to its attainment. For this model of adapting means to premeditated ends is one that haunts all our thinking about the promotion of what is valuable. In the educational sphere we therefore tend to look round for the equivalent of bridges to be built or ports to be steered to. Hence the complaints of lack of direction when obvious candidates do not appear to fill the bill.

It is my conviction that this model misleads us in the sphere of education. We have got the wrong picture of the way in which values must enter into education and this is what occasions the disillusioned muttering about the absence of agreed aims. But to bring out how we are misled we must look at the contexts where the means-end model *is* appropriate.

[1] From R. S. Peters, *Authority, Responsibility and Education.* London: George Allen & Unwin Ltd., 2nd edition, 1963, pp. 85-95. (With revisions in W. F. Frankena (ed.), *Philosophy of Education.* New York: The Macmillan Company, 1965, pp. 45-51.) Reprinted by permission of George Allen & Unwin Ltd. and Paul S. Eriksson, Inc.

There is, first of all, that of plans and purposes where we do things in order to put ourselves in the way of other things. We get on a bus in order to get to work; we fill up a form in order to get some spectacles. Our life is not just doing one thing after another; we impose plans and schedules on what we do by treating some as instrumental to others. Some of these we regard as more commendable than others, and what we call our scale of values bears witness to such choices. The second means-end context is that of making or producing things. We mix the flour in order to make a cake or weld steel in order to make a bridge. We speak of the end-product in a factory and of the means of production in an economic system.

In both these contexts we might well ask a person what he was aiming at, what his objective was. But in both cases the answer would usually be in terms of something pretty concrete. He might say something like 'getting a better job' or 'marrying the girl' in the first context; or something like 'producing a soundless aeroplane' in the second. Similarly if a teacher was asked what he was aiming at, he might state a limited objective like 'getting at least six children through the eleven-plus.' But he might, as it were, lift his eyes a bit from the scene of battle and commit himself to one of the more general aims of education—elusive things like 'the self-realization of the individual,' 'character,' 'wisdom,' or 'citizenship.' But here the trouble starts; for going to school is not a *means* to these in the way in which getting on a bus is a means of getting to work; and they are not made or produced out of the material of the mind in the way in which a penny is produced out of copper. These very general aims are neither goals nor are they end-products. Like 'happiness' they are high-sounding ways of talking about doing some things rather than others and doing them in a certain manner. From an ethical point of view it is crucial to examine the concrete style and content of the activities falling under such generalized aims, as well as the interpersonal rules which they involve.

It might be objected that education is an art like medicine and that in medicine there is a commonly accepted end-product—physical health. Why should there not be a similar one for education—mental health, for instance? The answer is fairly obvious. Doctors deal mainly with the body and if they agree about what constitutes physical health it is because it can be defined in terms of physical criteria like temperature level and metabolism rate. Also there is little objection to manipulating and tinkering with the body in order to bring about the required result.

In the case of education, however, there are no agreed criteria for defining mental health; for either it designates something purely negative like the absence of unconscious conflicts, or, in so far as it is a positive concept, it has highly disputable personal and social preferences written into it. Also education is not, like medicine or psychiatry, a remedial business.[2] When we are concerned with the minds of men there are objections to bringing about positive results in certain sorts of ways. People make moral objections to pre-frontal leucotomy even as a remedial measure. How much more objectionable would it be to promote some more positive state of mind, like a love of peace, in all men by giving them drugs or operating on everyone at birth? Indeed, in my view, disputes between educationists, which take the form of disputes about aims, have largely been disputes about the desirability of a variety of principles involved in such procedures. Values are involved in education not so much as goals or end-products, but as principles implicit in different manners of proceeding or producing. . . .

To illustrate more clearly the distinction which I am drawing between 'aims' and 'principles of procedure', let me take a parallel from politics. A man who believes in equality, might, like Godwin, be lured by a positive picture of a society in which differences between people would be minimized. He might want to get rid of differences in wealth and rank, even to breed people in the attempt to iron out innate differences. He might even go so far as to advocate the abolition of institutions like the army or the Church in which some men were given opportunities of lording it over others. Another social reformer, however, might employ the principle of equality in a much more negative sense without any concrete picture to lure him on his journey. He might insist, merely, that whatever social changes were introduced, no one should be treated differently from anyone else unless a good reason could be produced to justify such unequal treatment. The Godwin type of man would rightly be regarded as pursuing equality as a very general aim; the more cautious Liberal would have no particular aim connected with equality. He would merely insist that whatever schemes were put forward must not be introduced in a way which would infringe his procedural principle.

I think that this is an illuminating parallel to the point I am trying to make about the aims of education. For, in my view, many disputes about the aims of education are disputes about principles of procedure rather than about 'aims' in the sense of objectives to be arrived at by taking appropriate means. The so-called 'aims' in part pick out the different valuations which are built into the different procedures like training, instruction, the use of authority, teaching by example and rational

---

[2] For further discussion of this see R. S. Peters, "Mental Health as an Educational Aim," in *Aims of Education—The Philosophical Approach*, ed. T. Hollins (Manchester: University of Manchester Press, 1964).

explanation, all of which fall under the general concept of 'education'.

Consider, for instance, the classic dispute about the aims of education which is so often connected with an argument about the derivation of the word 'education'.[3] There were those like Sir Percy Nunn who stressed the connection with *educere*—to lead out. For them the aim of education must therefore be the development or realization of individual potentialities. Others, like Sir John Adams stressed the derivation from *educare*—to train, or mould according to some specification. They might be regarded as people who in fact believed in aims in a proper sense, in moulding boys into Christian gentlemen, for instance. The progressive who protests against this conception of education is not simply jibbing at the end-product of a Christian gentleman. He is also jibbing at the assimilation of education to an art where something is produced out of material. Rousseau, for instance, protested vociferously against treating children as little mannikins, as material to be poured into an adult mould. A child, he argued, should be treated with respect as a person. The progressive, therefore, like Dewey or Kilpatrick, presents another picture of the educational process. The child's interest must be awakened and he must be put into situations where the task rather than the man exerts the discipline. He will thus acquire habits and skills that are useful to him, and, by co-operating with others in common tasks, will develop respect for others and for himself. In the eyes of the progressive the use of authority as a principle of procedure is not only an inefficient way to pass on skills and information; it is also an immoral way to treat a child. It is made even worse in both respects by techniques like the use of reward and punishment.

So at the one end of the family tree generated by the concept of 'education' there are procedures involving the use of authority in which the voice and the cane are used to produce a desirable end-product. Education is here conceived in the image of fashioning an object in the arts. At the other end the importance of purposes and plans is stressed; but it is the purpose and planning of the child not of the adult. As Rousseau put it: 'By attempting nothing in the beginning you would have produced an educational prodigy.'

But, as any educationist must know, if he reflects on the matter, these are only a limited selection of the procedures that are in fact employed. There is, for instance, the influence exerted by one person on another in some sort of apprenticeship system, when the teacher guides

---

[3] For further discussion of the concept of "education" see R. S. Peters, "Education as Initiation," in *Philosophy of Education—A British View*, ed. R. Archambault (London: Routledge & Kegan Paul Ltd., 1964).

rather than goads. We learn carpentry by doing it with someone who is a bit better at carpentry; we learn to think clearly by talking with someone who thinks a bit more clearly than we do. And this other person need not be a charismatic figure so beloved by the advocates of 'impressionism' in the public schools or Boy Scout movement. It may be a person who is not only skilled but who has the additional ability of being able to explain and give an account of what he is up to. Progressives often object to talk and chalk and confuse the use of the voice with one way in which it is used—the authoritative way. But most good teachers use their voices to excite and to explain, not simply to instruct, command, or drill.

My guess is that most of the important things in education are passed on in this manner—by example and explanation. An attitude, a skill, is caught: sensitivity, a critical mind, respect for people and facts develop where an articulate and intelligent exponent is on the job. Yet the model of means to ends is not remotely applicable to the transaction that is taking place. Values, of course, are involved in the transaction: if they were not it would not be called 'education.' Yet they are not end-products or terminating points of the process. They reside both in the skills and cultural traditions that are passed on and in the procedure for passing them on. . . .

There are all sorts of things that can be passed on that are valuable. Almost anything, as I started off by saying, can be regarded as being of educational value. And, to a large extent, those who favour one type of procedure rather than another choose examples that suit themselves and advocate the practice of things that can be passed on best in accordance with their favourite model. The man who advocates authority and drill is most at home with things like Latin and arithmetic where rules have simply to be learnt defining what is right or wrong and where, in the early stages at any rate, there is little scope for rational explanation or learning by experience. The progressive is most at home with things like art, drama, and environmental studies where projects can develop without too much artificiality. And the man who believes in rational instruction is usually inclined toward things like science, history, and geometry. . . .

. . . Of course, many of the things which we do can be regarded as ways of implementing concrete and limited objectives. But this picture of the pursuit of aims is often exalted into grandiose talk about the purpose of life or the purpose of political activity. Self-realization, the greatest happiness of the greatest number, and the classless society act as lures to provide a distant destination for the great journey of life. Such general aims are not just harmless extravagances due to the overworking of a limited model of means to ends, a sort of metaphysical whistle in the dark. For men will do terrible things to other men in order to implement aims like racial purity which are both idiotic and illusory. The crucial question to ask, when men wax enthusiastic on the subject of their aims, is what *procedures* are to be adopted in order to implement them. We then get down to moral brass tacks. Do they in fact favour the model of implementing aims taken from the arts and from technology? There are those who favour the maximum of authoritative regulation such as is necessary in an army; there are those who use other people and mould them for their own purposes; there are those who are determined to live according to rational principles and to extend the maximum of toleration to others who disagree with them; there are those whose preoccupation is the pursuit of private good for whom hell is the other fellow.

These differences of procedure are writ large in the family, in economic affairs, and in political life. In education they are accentuated because the impact of man upon man is more conscious and because people are put into positions of authority where there is great scope for adopting their favoured procedures. My point is that arguments about the aims of education reflect these basic differences in principles of procedure. The Puritan and the Catholic both thought they were promoting God's kingdom, but they thought it had to be promoted in a different manner. And the different manner made it quite a different kingdom.

Of course arguments about general aims do not reflect *only* differences in principles of procedure or disagreements about the relative importance of public needs and individual development. Equally important are valuations of content where the merits of, e.g. art as distinct from those of science or history are under discussion. But the real issues involved in such comparisons are obscured by talk about self-realization, life, happiness, and so on. For what sort of self is to be realized? What quality of life is worth perpetuating? Teachers surely care whether or not poetry rather than push-pin is perpetuated, to use a time-honoured example. The problem of justifying such 'higher' activities is one of the most difficult and persistent problems in ethics. But talk about self-realization and other such omnibus 'ends' does more than obscure it; it also encourages an *instrumental* way of looking at the problem of justification. For a nebulous end is invented which such activities are supposed to lead up to, because it is erroneously assumed that education must be justified by reference to an end which is extrinsic to it. The truth is much more that there is a quality of life embedded in the activities which constitute education, and that 'self-realization' can be explicated only by reference to such activities. Thus, if by 'life' is meant what goes on outside schools and universities, there is an important sense in which 'life' must be for the sake of education, not education for life.

R. S. Peters: Aims of Education[1]

I have argued elsewhere[2] that much of the confusion about aims of education' comes about through extracting the normative feature built into the concept of 'education' as an extrinsic end. Given that 'education' suggests the intentional bringing about of a desirable state of mind in a morally unobjectionable manner, it is only too easy to conceive of education as a neutral process that is instrumental to something that is worthwhile which is extrinsic to it. Just as gardens may be cultivated in order to aid the economy of the household, so children must be educated in order to provide them with jobs and to increase the productivity of the community as a whole.

But there is something inappropriate about this way of speaking; for we would normally use the word 'train' when we had such a specifiable extrinsic objective in mind. If, however, we do specify an appropriate 'aim' such as the development of individual potentialities or the development of intellect and character, then the aim would be intrinsic to what we would consider education to be. For we would not call a person 'educated' who had not developed along such lines. It would be like saying that the aim of reform is to develop an individual's sense of responsibility. This would give content to our understanding of making a man better, which is what it means to reform him, just as the development of intellect and character gives content to the notion of developing what is worth while, which is what it means to educate someone. If a dispute started about such 'aims'—e.g. whether a sense of responsibility was more important than respect for others or whether the development of intellect was more important than the development of character — this would not be a dispute about ends which were extrinsic to reform or education; rather it would be a dispute about what was the most important characteristic of a reformed or educated man. Such aims mark out specific achievements and states of mind that give content to the formal notion of 'the educated man'.

Another way of arriving at the same point is by an examination of the concept of 'aim'. The term 'aim' has its natural home in the con-

---

[1] From R. S. Peters, *Ethics and Education*. London: George Allen & Unwin Ltd., 1966, pp. 27-30, with omissions. Reprinted by permission of George Allen & Unwin Ltd.

[2] See R. S. Peters, *Education as Imitation* (London: Evans Bros., 1963).

text of limited and circumscribed activities like shooting and throwing. 'Aiming' is associated with the concentration of attention within such an activity on some object which must be hit, or pierced. Its internal accusative 'target' covers anything conforming to this specification. When the term 'aim' is used more figuratively it has the same suggestion of the concentration of attention on something which is the focus of an activity. It is odd to use it like the term 'purpose' or 'motive' to suggest some explanatory end for the activity in question. We can reasonably ask a person what his purpose is in building a new house or his motive in visiting a sick friend when we want to know what he sees these activities as leading up to; but it would be odd to ask for the *aim* of these activities, if we wanted to remove our puzzlement about their explanation. To ask for an aim is to ask for a more precise specification of what an action or activity is. We ask people what they are aiming at when they seem rather confused about their purposes or when they are drawing up a plan of campaign and have to formulate what they intend to do in a coherent way. Asking a person about his aims is a method of getting him to concentrate or clear his mind about what he is trying to do. 'Aim' also carries the suggestion that we are trying to achieve something that we might fall short of because of the difficulty involved in the task. Targets are things which we have to concentrate on if we want to hit them; so too, when we talk figuratively about what we are aiming at, we intimate the possibility of missing or falling short. If we say to someone 'What are you aiming at doing?' instead of 'What do you intend to do?' this is a quaint colloquialism which carries the suggestion both of concentration and of the possibility of falling short.

It is obvious enough, therefore, why the term 'aim' is used so frequently in the context of education. For this is a sphere where people engage with great seriousness in activities without always being very clear about what they are trying to achieve, and where genuine achievements are difficult to come by. To ask questions about the aims of education is therefore a way of getting people to get clear about and focus their attention on what is worth while achieving. It is not to ask for the production of ends extrinsic to education which might explain their activities as educators. Aims can be high level or low level. A teacher can write down in his lesson notes that his aim in the coming lesson is to reach the end of Exercise 6, or to get his pupils to speak some Latin, or grasp something about ancient Rome. Or he may say his aim is to train their character a bit by making them cope with a difficult unseen. But, whatever he says he is aiming at, the formulation of his aim is an aid to making his activity more structured and coherent by isolating an aspect under which he is acting. It is not something which he does in order to explain what he is doing; it is, rather, a more precise specification of it.

The natural way of asking for an extrinsic end is to ask what a man's purpose is in doing something or what his motive for it may be. These are strange questions to ask about education itself, for as 'education' implies the transmission of what is of ultimate value, it would be like asking about the purpose of the good life; but they are reasonable questions to ask about the activities that fall under education. For things like science and carpentry can be practised and passed on both for their own intrinsic value and because of the contribution which they make to extrinsic ends such as productivity, housing, and health. But in so far as they are regarded as part of someone's *education* they are regarded *ipso facto* as having value, and therefore as having reasons for being built into education, which he comes to accept. Confusion about aims of education often derives from saying things about education itself which are appropriate when said about activities which can be and usually are regarded as having educational value.

Rubin Gotesky: Means, Ends-in-View, Anticipations and Outcomes [1]

John Dewey in *Experience and Nature* distinguished between "end" and "end-in-view." Dewey made this distinction in order to expose the strong tendency to confuse a *desired* termination with an *actual* termination. My purpose in using this distinction of Dewey's is to elaborate a schema of concepts which might make a beginning at the rational testing and validation of ends-in-view. The schema developed below may show that ends-in-view, when treated in a certain way, are also testable.

I shall not try to establish that men are end-in-viewers or planful creatures. I take this as an empirical fact; and I believe there is sufficient evidence available to convince even the most doubtful of its truth. I am not saying that man is planful in every thing he does, but that he is planful in much that he does. Further, I am accepting as fact that man's planfulness is a causal element in producing a certain kind of future, whether this future be catastrophic or beneficial to himself. Lastly, I accept as fact that man changes his ends-in-view, in many cases, in the light of evidence. My schema is intended to reveal the way in which evidence can and seems to affect man's views of his ends-in-view.

[1] From *Educational Theory*. Urbana: University of Illinois, vol. XIII, no. 2, 1963, pp. 85-90, with omissions. Reprinted by permission of *Educational Theory* and Rubin Gotesky.

I shall not follow Dewey's distinction between "end" and "end-in-view" exactly, nevertheless I want to emphasize, as he did, that our experiences have *beginnings* and *ends,* i.e., ends in the sense of terminations", "conclusions", "culminations". And I want further to emphasize, as he did, that ends, in the sense of "terminations", do not necessarily involve desires, purposes, or preferences. In fact, even if desires, purposes or preferences were present, ends in the sense of terminations need be neither preferred, purposed nor desired. They may, in fact, be what is *not* preferred, purposed or desired. Ends as terminations are simply the last events or the last sets of events occurring in a sequence of events.

"End" as "end-in-view" differs first of all from termination in that it has not yet occurred. It is a termination-to-occur not *merely* in the sense that it has not as yet occurred, but in the sense that it may *never* occur. Secondly, end-in-view is more than simply a future termination, for any termination, in terms of time, can have a past, present or future. To be an end-in-view, this future termination must be a concern, an interest, of some creature capable of anticipation and of anticipating it. Without this concern or interest and anticipation, there is no end-in-view. In saying it is a concern or an interest of some creature, we mean that it is something desired or not desired, wanted or rejected. Thirdly, to be an end-in-view, it must be a termination which the intended actions or behavior of the end-viewing creature can bring or—at least—which it believes it can by some sequence of controlled actions bring about.

Even if the termination is in the future and of concern to some living creature, it is still *not* an end-in-view. For example, the rising of the moon may be both in the future and a matter of concern to some living creature, yet it may not be an end-in-view, since it is not something which any living creature known to us can bring about by some controlled action or sequence of controlled actions. Of course, some living creature may wrongly believe that its actions do bring about some termination. In that case, even though the creature is mistaken, the future termination may be said to be an end-in-view.

Finally, an end-in-view is *not necessarily* a purpose. We wish to restrict the word, "purpose", to those ends-in-view which include some kind of rational justification. Ends-in-view which are of concern or of interest, desired, wanted, sought after, are not as such purposes. They are simply matters of concern or interest. For example, to want an apple is an end-in-view, but it may not, in our mode of talking, be called a purpose unless—and this is the important point—it involves some kind of justification such as wanting an apple because it has a particular taste quality, say, a sweet acidity which is not found in other edible fruits.

A word of Caution! In speaking of end-in-view as a future termination, a termination-to-occur, I want to repeat again that I do not want to be understood as saying that the termination, by the actions of some living creature, will eventually be brought into being. Termination as end-in-view is something simply in a creature's eye, a gleam, a hope, an expectation of something desired to occur or not to occur. However strong may be the want and the effort made, the termination may never occur and no creature may be able to make it occur, ever. However, insofar as some living creature has such a termination in mind, it inevitably appears as something that can be made to occur at some time in the future. It is important to emphasize this difference between end-in-view and termination; and so to make more certain that I am understood, I want to re-express this difference in another way. Terminations are actual occurrences or sequences of occurrences; they are the final events or set of events in a specially related larger set of events. But ends-in-view are *not* actual occurrences or actual sequences of occurrences. They are imaginations or projections by some living creature of non-existent terminations which that creature wishes to make actual or to prevent from becoming actual. To illustrate, some person wishes to be a millionaire. "Being a millionaire" is not for this person an actual state of affairs. It is an imagination, a projection of his wish into the future. Despite every effort, his wish as end-in-view may never be actualized.

Ends-in-view are of several kinds; and we shall attempt to describe and exemplify those kinds which seem to us important for our purpose. The first kind we shall call "objectives." An "objective" is an end-in-view which has the following characteristics:

1. The end-in-view is relatively simple like wanting an apple or a typewriter. It is simple in two respects: a) there is no difficulty in knowing what is wanted or is of concern and b) what is wanted is not easily confused with any other end-in-view. The distinction between a) and b) can be illustrated in this way. If an apple were wanted, a) it would not be a rotten, unedible apple. In other words, the wanter would know the kind of apple he wants. b) He would not confuse the kind he wants with any other kind. If he wanted an apple and did not know the kind he wanted, his end-in-view would not so far be an objective.

2. The means required to attain the end-in-view are small in number and easily ordered as to efficacy i.e., in producing the desired termination. For example, the means for getting an apple are relatively few: a food market which sells apples; money to buy; a convenient vehicle to reach the food market; secondly entering the food market to obtain the apple; and lastly paying in currency to complete the economic exchange.

3. The time required for achieving the end-in-view is small.

Even though objectives can be well defined, it does not follow that they always are. Often enough, they are left unclear, unspecified, primarily because of ignorance or sloth. Objectives can always be well formulated. Again, that they can be well-formulated does not necessarily mean that they are achievable. Often enough, they may be intrinsically not achievable; but with the sort of ends-in-view which we call objectives, it is fairly easy to discover why. It may be that the means used are not satisfactory. For example, one wants a high polish to one's shoes; one believes that rubbing with a handkerchief will achieve this. The act of rubbing one's shoes with a handkerchief will soon reveal whether the means are adequate or not. Or it may be that certain conditions or states of affairs are absent. For example, a student lacks the intelligence to understand numbers, a condition presumably necessary for mastering numbers.

Objectives tend, under given conditions, to nucleate, to cluster together, to form more or less complex or compound sets. This occurs as a result of two conditions: a) when objectives are related to each other in time in such a way that the attainment of one objective depends upon the attainment of another; (This relation I call "objectival dependency.") and b) when a number of objectives are together found to be essential for the attainment of one or more objectives. (This sort of situation I call "objectival co-incidence.")

I call such nucleations or clusters of objectives, both dependent and coincidental, "goals." Examples of such goals are the mastering of elementary physics or logic or attaining a career, say, that of becoming a doctor, an engineer, or the "goal" of winning a war.

"Goals" are distinguished from objectives (1) in being highly complex, (2) in that the means required are numerous, not easily ordered, not easily obtained, and not easily usable and (3) in requiring considerable periods of time to achieve them. Because goals are complex and require long periods of time to achieve them—if they are achievable, there is always strong uncertainty that they can be achieved and that the means required are available for achievement. Often enough, conditions change; conditions which were present and necessary at the time the goal was elected, disappear. In the course of attempting to attain the goal, the goal may lose its original desirability or importance. The labor and effect involved; the frustrations, disappointments, absence of essential means, the necessity again and again to improvise new means; the inclusion of new objectives into the goal structure—may altogether destroy the desirability of or need for the goal long before it is even in sight or at its termination-point. Consequently goals unlike objectives cannot be so clearly formulated. They possess an essential imprecision; a vagueness both in the process of attainment and in the attainment itself.

Goals unlike objectives usually change in essential respects. New experiences, new conditions usually involve the inclusion of new objectives. For example, the goal of becoming a teacher in elementary school has changed radically since the days of the little red school house. Teachers today need to master such subjects as child psychology, pedagogic methods, curriculum planning, subjects and skills which were not part of the required objectives to be attained by the little red school house teacher of not so long ago. Moreover the goal today of becoming a teacher at any level constantly undergoes modification, i.e., new objectives are included and old objectives excluded every few years. And this is today true for nearly all highly skilled professions like medicine, law, engineering, etc.

Like objectives, goals, too, tend to nucleate, to cluster together. But by nucleating, by clustering together, goals yield a new kind of end-in-view which I call "ideals". Ideals interrelate goals and objectives in terms of wide-range and long-time terminations. Further they express the purposes, for which goals and objectives came into being or were created. They orientate individuals, groups, institutions and societies in terms of what is permissible and impermissible, do-able and not do-able. Consequently ideals are extremely complex and invariably ambiguous. They are constantly the source of divisions of opinion, public controversy and even bloody struggle.

It is not easy to clarify the logical relations of ideals to goals and objectives. For example, it is apparently still impossible to establish an incontrovertible logical relation between the goals which men seek and such ideals as Democracy, Christianity or Communism. To Marxists, goals like being a doctor or an engineer are better served under the ideal of Communism. To Democrats or Christians, such goals are better served under the respective ideals of Democracy or Christianity. So ambiguous are the logical relations of goals to ideals that even those who purport to agree about ideals do not agree about the way goals are related to them.

Ideals define the purposes of goals and goal-clusters. They justify the activities leading to their attainment and the activities following from their attainment. Thus the goal of a doctor is that of *becoming* a doctor, but it also involves *being* a doctor. The ideal answers the question: "What is the reason, the justification, for becoming and being a doctor?" Ideals, in other words, state for what or why something is being done. Ideals are always implicit in goals, but they tend to be made more and more explicit as goals tend to cluster together, to relate themselves to each other in some sort of order, both sequential and coincidental.

Ideals also have levels. There are first the ideals which derive directly from and justify the goals sought by individuals, institutions or societies. These ideals we shall call Ideal $_1$. The goal of becoming a doctor is intrinsically justified in terms of preserving the health and life of mankind. This is an example of Ideal $_1$. However, such an ideal tends to become generalized so that it turns into an ideal for all sorts of diverse activities. A lawyer—whatever may be the specific ideal of law—must not do anything destructive of the health and life of mankind. And this ideal applies as well to the teacher, the dentist, the carpenter, the street cleaner. All who somehow act in such a way as to destroy health and life act wrongly. When generalized, Ideal $_1$ attains the level of what I call Ideal $_2$—i.e., an ideal which gives a rationale, a justification for a variety of goals or objectives.

Ideals of type Ideal $_2$ tend to nucleate or cluster into something I prefer to call "the-ideal", a hyphenation of "the" and "ideal", and which Kant preferred to call the "Kingdom of Ends". For me, there is not, as with Kant, just one such "the-idea"; there are many such as for example the "the-ideals" of Democracy, Christianity, Communism or Anarchism. Even within each of these "the-ideals", there are different, in part overlapping and in part incompatible, the-ideal versions. But all the-ideals have a common function: *that of interrelating all objectives, goals, and ideals into a common order, structure or system....*

*   *   *   *

... These three kinds of ends-in-view exist together, evolve from and involve each other in manifold and diverse ways. Ideals may, under given conditions, generate new goals or repudiate old ones; goals can generate either new ideals or objectives or lead to the rejection of old ideals and objectives. Objectives, in turn, can alter goals or ideals or even lead to their rejection.

8

Review—On the Aimer and His Aim

The two complementary functions of this final chapter are first to review, and second to evaluate. The three-fold approach of analysis and classification, illustration, and theory can now be brought together in a single perspective on aims in education. None of these is sufficient in itself. Indeed, there is evidence that the question of aims may even be clouded by an exclusive preoccupation with one of them, such as analysis of concepts. For however useful analysis may be toward clarification, its abstractions are apt to be misunderstood unless the reader is prepared to restore them, by reflection, to the current of his own experience. Thus, in order to emphasize his objection to extrinsic ends for the very reason that they are extracted from experience, Peters argues that there is a normative feature built into the concept of "education."[1]

By implication, if one mentions "education" one conveys at once both the notion of an activity that is worthwhile and the notion of aiming. The arbitrariness of this position stems from its concentration on selected usages of "education" rather than on all possible usages, a focusing on concepts of "liberal education" and "moral education." (It is arguable, indeed, that if "education" itself implies worthwhileness, then adjectives applied to it such as "liberal" and "moral" are redundant.) Just as analysis abstracts from experience, for a balanced perspective

---

[1] *Ethics and Education,* op. cit., pp. 27, 29. Also, "What is an Educational Process?" in *The Concept of Education.* London: Routledge and Kegan Paul, Ltd., 1967, pp. 4-5.

on the educational process its distinctions need to be restored to experience.

To return to Peters' argument that the concept of "education" is itself normative, or has value built into it, it is understandable that some should infer from this that the entire area of aims in education is redundant, that aims can be taken for granted once one has grasped the fundamental concept of "education." This anthology has set out to present a contrary viewpoint. To bring together its various sections in a single focus is to see that aims in education can be clarified by analysis and classification, by illustration, and by theoretical enquiry.

To clarify recorded aims in Parts I-III, the main questions asked were: How do aims function in experience? Are the aims readily attainable? and Are the aims self-made and self-oriented (personal), or are they made by others and other-oriented (external)? Toward a clearer understanding of aim-statements by the theoretical approach in the preceding chapter, the same questions were again asked, as well as the more specific, What does one *mean* by educational aims?

The combined effect of asking all of these questions has been to expose certain aspects of educational aims that call for special comment or explanation. These aspects relate first, to the structuring of aims and to the means-end relationship; second, to the problem of extrinsic ends as part of a structure of aims; third, to philosophical preconceptions; fourth, to semantic sources of vagueness in aim statements; and fifth, to personal choices and group choices. The first three of these are closely interrelated.

The structuring of aims and the means-end relationship

On the question of whether aims can be structured in any way in terms of constant means-end relationships, and particularly whether any ends can be held to be ultimate, stable, or absolute, this anthology has shown that among educational philosophers there is a disagreement which has its source partly in a situational point of view and partly in philosophical assumptions. However, regardless of one's philosophical premises or preconceptions—which will be separately considered—one may look at educational aims from two distinct points of view: experientially and normatively.

Looking from the experiential point of view one would concur entirely with the argument that the status of an aim may change with a change of situation. From this viewpoint who would not agree that (a) the organization of pupils' reports in a class project is a means to (b) the end of extending participation in discussion, which is a means to (c) the end of improving clarity of communication, and that this flexibility of means-end adjustment admits even of the reversibility of (c) becoming a means to (b), and (b) a means to (a)?

Again, there is a clear fluidity of means and ends in the following case: A teacher narrates a selected life-story to pupils as a means of developing an understanding of their heritage. He then uses this understanding of heritage as a means of forming dispositions of respect for past achievements. In turn, he sees their dispositions of respect for past achievements as means to an increased knowledge of their heritage. In Heraclitean terms, just as one cannot step twice into the same river, so one cannot identify any means or ends as always means or ends at different points of the river's course. Related to concrete situations, this much is simple: one is looking at the flow before one's eyes, not at the river toward the end of its course. A person may be preoccupied, as Dewey was, with observing and perhaps modifying the current in which he is temporarily engaged. And though not with any final end in view, he will certainly still take account of what has flowed from the past, and will be ever mindful of the way he would like the current of experience to flow in the future.

To this point one is impelled to agree with Dewey, but the position Dewey could not sustain was that this is the *only* intelligent point of view on educational aims. Specifically, he could not establish that such an intelligent point of view precludes a view of the way one would *like* the river to flow, not merely when it is out of immediate sight but also, and even contrary to the evidence of the present and the past, when it carries individuals to maturity. For Dewey permitted himself the indulgence of an end that was both enticing and imperfectly attainable, an end remote and out of reach but devoutly to be desired. His was an end of a perfect democracy. Thus, it was only at the risk of inconsistency that Dewey could deny ultimates among educational aims. Conceptually an ultimate formed part of his fabric of thought, and however staunchly he advocated a concentration on things that mattered in the stream of experience and on things that would make a difference in actual living, he could not escape from his two distinct viewpoints: one empirical, the other normative. And it seems that this ambivalence belongs to most people who ponder the aims of education, however much they may accent one viewpoint for their own immediate purposes. The ultimates Dewey wished to preclude, because in his judgment they made no difference to the stream of individual experience, were ultimates of a very special kind which may now be briefly considered.

Extrinsic ends

Although appreciating the difficulty of demolishing any system of thought for its inclusion of remote ends, ideals, or ultimates—since these as such are not incompatible with points of view that focus on current human events and their intelligent modifiability—one finds it much less difficult to challenge in experience the notion of a structuring of aims which proceeds invariably from simple to complex to remote, and which postulates ends extrinsic to the educational process. For the objection Dewey raised had some weight: it was traditionally unrecognized by those who postulated extrinsic ends that their attainability was guaranteed on grounds of personal belief, not on grounds of empirical evidence. And by their nature, beliefs on ultimate ends that are conceived of as belonging to a world outside that of everyday experience not only differ, but sometimes also conflict in ways that tend to reflect on their probability.

This argument applies to ends that are romantic extrapolations from experience as much as to ends that are supernaturally based. All extrinsic ends by definition lie outside the stream of everyday experience, and for that very reason invoke common criticisms. One of these is that it is difficult to relate a world of experience to a world outside experience. For instance, it is frequently considered that a complex disposition of critical thinking is the justification for the simple objective of a knowledge of some common informal fallacies of argument, for both of these ends-in-view belong to everyday experience and share a common intelligibility for that reason. However, it is only rarely considered that a remote objective of an ideal democracy is the justification for a complex disposition of critical thinking, for now there are two worlds involved—ideal and natural—and the limited intelligibility of the first deprives it of immediacy and directness in influencing the second.

Another objection is that the extrinsic aim has a habit of becoming associated with a structuring of objectives. As an end-product or an ultimate, the extrinsic aim is elevated to the highest status in a hierarchical order. Yet a sequential and hierarchical relationship is clearly not a necessary condition for the realization of any particular objective. For instance, one may attain a specific simple objective, such as a knowledge of the length of the Hudson River, without relating it to anything either complex or ideal. And one may aspire to attain a form of perfectly altruistic democratic citizenship quite independently of the fulfillment of any specific objective. Somewhat paradoxically a preoccupation with hierarchies of aims is frequently a preconception of "ultimates," so that the remote objective is not what it sometimes purports to be in an individual's thought; it is the *beginning* rather than the *end* of a process. The ordering of aims carries with it a suggestion of an irreversibility of objectives that is not consistent with experience, and a suggestion of a rigidity that is imposed to justify a kind of super-end extrinsic to the process.

Yet, is it clear what "extrinsic" as opposed to "intrinsic" is? While it might be readily agreed that some of the formulated "ultimates" among educational aims lie outside the educational process, other ultimates raise questions of definition and of belief. The assertion that the ultimate aim of education is to make the human spirit closer to the Divine Mind, or God, may be construed by some as intrinsic to the process of education, and by others as extrinsic both to the process and to any known or knowable human experience. It is at this point that some statements of educational aims are shown to be supportable only by reference to basic philosophical assumptions.

Philosophical Preconceptions

If one divides the world of educational aim-makers into two contrasting camps, the sharpest distinctions may be drawn between extreme confrontations of naturalism and supernaturalism, empiricism and metaphysics. To what extent are these distinctions valid? It is clear that the connotation of "extrinsic" has become narrower. It is no longer used for experiential ideals that are extrinsic to experience in the sense that they grow out of it and stand, like Dewey's ideal democracy, as models of Platonic ideas. Rather is it confined now to two related senses with their sources in the supernatural: to beliefs in a world of values independent of, and superior to, the natural world of imperfections; and to ends such as affinity with Divine Mind, whose fulfillment can refer only to a world outside the world of everyday experience, however much one may believe in human potentiality to progress toward that end. The crux of the matter is this: some beliefs—even beliefs in the supernatural—are applied in educational aim-making only to the modification of everyday experience, whereas other beliefs are invariably oriented toward supernatural ends. It is the latter which in a sense divert attention from the quality of experience in the natural world and the continued improvement of this experience by educational means.

To give point to the contrast, there are supernaturally-based beliefs on ends such as rational development, good character, the good life, personal fulfillment whose premises permit of partial attainment in the natural world. With perfection unattained and unattainable, the vision always lies beyond experience, just as it does in the case of ideal democracy. In all such instances the nature of the impact on educational aim-making, and on the educational process as a whole, is not vitally affected by the nature of the premises, whether they are naturalistic or supernaturalistic. Each has its genesis in an impulse to improve experience, and thus the concentration of attention is on education for life. It may be said that the model justifies the activities advocated. Hutchins has an ideal of rational perfection based on supernatural premises of reason as a divine gift to man and on man's unchanging nature. From these beliefs he deduces an educational program of rigorous intellectual training, aimed at discovering truth by reading the thoughts of the greatest minds from a selection of the outstanding books of all times. In contrast, though, there are others with supernatural premises whose visions extend beyond the practicalities of educational experience to ends that belong essentially to another world. Some find it difficult to understand, for instance, how educators could ever *know how* to guide pupils toward an absolute end of likeness to the spiritual order of the universe as an infinite personal ideal. It appears, therefore, that it is not the supernatural premises *as such* that divert attention from the quality of educational experience, but rather metaphysical generalities that one has no means of fathoming by resort to any of the intellectual tools within one's grasp.

Semantic sources of vagueness in aim statements

There are many sources of linguistic vagueness which are common to aim-statements. The word "aim," that one might expect to symbolize something straight-forward and directive, is sometimes distorted by emotion, persuasiveness, and irrelevance. Other sources of vagueness are conceptual, and language is powerless to sharpen their clarity. The metaphysical statement is the most beguiling of these—especially as it is often made with zeal and fervor—for the very reason that it is so often pitched beyond the possibility of challenge or refutation by any logical or empirical examination. If the ultimate end of all education is said to be kinship with a universal spirit, and if this end is supported by such mystical elaborations as, "It will take all the time there is for the infinite fully to fill the finite, and the finite can have no richer objective for itself than to realize the infinite,"[1] inquiry reaches a stalemate. Maritain holds the end of education to be concerned with "personal life and spiritual progress," relating it to man's "spiritual superexistence" and to an innermost essence, "a mysterious identity which is a hidden thing that no techniques can reach."[2] With similar religious intensity, Buber baffles semantic inquiry with assertions that the educator's task is to put man again "face to face with God," but only the educator who is sensitive to the "wing-beat of the spirit and the creative word" will succeed.[3]

Each of these is an extreme form of supernaturalist statement, and it is worth observing further that not all metaphysical statements of the kind that frustrate attempts to examine their truth or falsity are of supernatural orientation. The inquiring mind would be almost as baffled by purely naturalistic claims that the ultimate aim of education is to promote freedom, or to nourish society, or to promote the cause of civilization.

Personal choice and group choices

The misleading nature of metaphor has been illustrated in the preceding remarks on the river of experience, a figure that can be manipulated to serve whatever purpose one has in mind. A concept of a single current of experience in which all contemporaries are somehow involved is a distortion of experience, for what contributes so strongly to the fluidity of experience is the very uniqueness of individuality, the fact that everyone has his own specific desires and ends-in-view, his own particular way of looking at the world, and his own personal current of experience, whatever connections it might have with the experiences of others.

The first premise to assert, then, is the principle of unique indi-

---

[1] H. H. Horne, "An Idealistic Philosophy of Education," *National Society for the Study of Education,* Yearbook XLI, Part I, University of Chicago Press, 1942.
[2] *Education at the Crossroads, op. cit.,* pp. 8-9.
[3] *Between Man and Man, op. cit.,* pp. 146-147.

viduality. The second is the principle of individual choice. Together these principles place serious restrictions on two common assumptions: the assumption that aims formulated by educators for imposition on pupils will "take"; and the assumption that groups, particularly small groups, can by mutual interaction of members form group goals that are uniformly transformed to personal goals.

On premises of individuality and of individual choice, the practice of prescribing an educational end for others can be successful, therefore, only in proportion to the success of the educator in persuading his pupils to accept the prescribed end as a personal end-in-view. If the aim remains external to the pupils' perceptions, it is properly not an aim since no one may be actively pursuing it. It may be as inert, indeed, as Croce's conception of mere chronicle that has failed to become living history. Yet one of the paradoxes of the educational process is that some external ends are necessarily prescribed by educators who, for the sake of economy and by virtue of their professional research knowledge and experience, make a selection of ends—in terms of knowledge, skills, attitudes, and understandings—consistent with *their* view of the world. These ends may be specific and immediate, as in defining subject-matter boundaries in history or social studies for particular grades; or they may be normative and complex, based on preconceptions of the sort of dispositions an individual should form; or they may be largely remote and speculative, based on patterns of particular beliefs. In every instance their efficacy is restricted to whatever success is attainable by a form of extrinsic motivation.

The extent of personal awareness of educational aims other than the simple is not assessable, but by considering a range of published objectives one may wonder how many generalized abstractions are assimilated within pupils' respective value systems, and how many are merely glimpsed as worthy objectives in fleeting moments of inspirational teaching. The possible delusions of certain sophisticated educators are not so evident in respect to short-range objectives, but in every instance it is clear that goal acceptance is, in the last resort, an individual matter.

In group situations the individual's recognition of an aim is never a guarantee of the aim's acceptance. Beyond conceptual grasp, goal acceptance implies a process of assimilation whereby an end that was once seen as alien or external to the value system is accommodated willingly within it. Both interest and satisfaction come by pursuing the aim for the very reason that it is something anticipated and personally desired. Any step by step systematization of the process of personal involvement in an aim is bound to be arbitrary and oversimplified because it overlooks the uniqueness of the individual and of his value system. When one considers individuals thinking and learning, either assimilating aims from others' aim-statements or formulating their own aims, even the concept of a continuum is inadequate to convey the great variety of possible two-way patterns of progression and regression that may occur. And there is difference rather than standardization not only in the aims individuals have, but also in the way they perceive their aims. A single objective such as memorization of a poem may be shared by a number of pupils, yet to say that they have the same objective is to conceal within a generality each one's different perception of the task ahead of him. In this sense the verbal statement of an objective can never hope to describe the state of mind of any individual as he accepts the objective. Abstractions such as "internalization" of aims are to this extent misleading. There is no single experience of internalization, for if it means simply a measure of personal acceptance, it has no uniform successive stages; if it implies something more than personal acceptance, it is in danger of invoking Gilbert Ryle's criticism of the ghost in the machine of the body.[1] There is no inner force of internalization which enables objectives to be perceived more clearly or welded more cohesively than by ordinary processes of thought. Yet, vague as they are, such concepts as internalization serve a useful function of stressing the foolishness of prescribing aims for others without serious consideration of the likelihood of their being individually assimilated.

* * * *

One of the perspectives gained by now looking back on the selections and by assuming their representativeness in educational literature, is of a disproportionate concentration of attention on ends *aimed at,* and among these a disproportionate emphasis placed on ends that *ought* to be aimed at and that are assumed to be aimed at by somebody standing apart from the learning situation. The combined effect of these normative and external observer viewpoints is that much that has been written on educational aims has been by those who have had no means of know-

[1] *The Concept of Mind.* London: Hutchinson, 1949, p. 15.

ing precisely whether or not the aims in question are ever realized or are indeed realizable.

Excluding the readily attainable simple objectives, readers are prone to see much of the remaining literature on educational aims as belonging to a nebulous zone of inconsequential and unpractical theorizing. How can this stigma be removed? The error has been to focus on the end of the process before giving due consideration to the beginning, to ignore the aimer and his aim and to assume that the aimer can always be briefed on what to aim at by those somehow better qualified to know. The normative educational aim-maker may be said to have an obligation to try to see his external formulations through the eyes of those for whom they are intended, and then, if a measure of empathy can be achieved, to set about organizing and supervising the means whereby his originally other-oriented objectives are likely to be transformed as rapidly as possible to self-oriented, or personal, pupil goals. And perhaps it is best that the conscience of the external air-maker be consistently exposed to the gad-fly stings of two questions: How do you *know* what is in the best interests of others? and, How can you get others to *accept* your assertion that your aims for them *are* in their best interests?

To begin at the beginning is to consider the aimer and his aim. Again metaphor intrudes, and again with misleading tendency. When the target image is used it implies that the aimer is finished with his task once he hits the target, unless practice for skill acquisition requires repetition of the operation. Such repetition among educational aimers is relevant only to short-range simple objectives, but *never* is the target-hitting properly an end in itself. Similarly, there is little aptness in describing educational objectives as hurdles to jump or ladders to climb, because once one is over the last hurdle or at the top of the ladder, one's significant educational activities cease. No strictly educational aim is of this kind. From the point of view of the learner the sense of continuity and the inter-relationships of learning tasks are both lost in the respective metaphors. The images mislead by forcing attention away from the beginning of the educational process to a supposed end. Even the signpost that supposedly gives direction mentions only the destination.

In the case of dispositional objectives, no target is ever hit, no last hurdle jumped, no ladder climbed to the topmost rung. No point in time ever arrives when one can rub one's hands with relief or satisfaction, assured that the job is finally done. There is probably no individual disposition which is identical in all complex cognitive and emotional respects from one day to the next. One is in a region of awareness where there is never any question of final destination. It is a question rather of a person keeping something up, of continuing with his attitude or interest, of trying to strengthen it. The focus must always be on the aimer and his individual aim, for although two persons might achieve an identical simple objective of learning a multiplication table, no two persons are likely to achieve an identical complex disposition or ever know what it would be like to aim at a specific disposition. More than ever in the case of dispositions, it is imperative to re-orient the literature of educational aims away from exclusive attention to ends toward the fundamental importance of the individual uniqueness of the aimer.

Dispositional objectives merge into ideals or remote aims. Generally they are the two sides of one coin: the one side perfection, the other the limits of attainability. Remote as they are to some, ideals serve as inspirations to others as they progress individually toward dispositional achievement. The efficacy of ideals in experience depends on individual motivation, and it becomes evident again that the uniqueness of the aimer and his aim is fundamental.

Is it assertable, then, that the educator or educationist can set up aims for others? Can he show the aimer how to aim and what to aim at? In any precise sense, the answer must be this: only in the case of simple objectives of particular knowledge, skills, and understanding can others be shown something of the technique of aiming and of what to aim at, but even in these cases, because of the privacy of mind, the educator can only infer the nature of the pupil's aim or whether, in fact, he has one. In the case of dispositions there is nothing clearly definable to aim at, nothing describable in an objective sense. What is to be aimed at is subjective, made by the learner himself, though perhaps influenced by models or examples or even exhortations. As with dispositions, so with ideals: no one can aim for the learner, no one can give him an aim, no one can show him precisely what to aim at. There can be no more than influences bearing on him.

On first impressions, to ignore the aimer and the act of aiming is an affront to human individuality, and for anyone to assert what another's educational goals should be savors of an arrogant denial of individual freedom. But when one asks, "From whom is the individual to be free? it becomes clear that there can be no such thing as absolute freedom for the individual in society, even in respect to his education. State regulation both curbs and protects individual freedom, and it is the interdependence of individuals, rather than their independence of one another, that is central to the very concept of society. Thus, there is a place for guidance as well as a place for personal aim-making. It is appropriate to learn from others as well as to learn independently of others: there is a time to listen to others, as well as a time to speak up for oneself.

The well-intentioned attempt of an educator to impose aims on others is not so much a violation of liberty as a violation of logic and of psychology. Every such educational aim-maker falls into the *prescriptive error:* the error of writing aims for others on the assumption that those others will certainly accept them. Inherent in this practice is a failure to understand the logic of aiming as distinct from the logic of aim-making. No one can prescribe for others a set of symbols that will necessarily be transformed to an aim. All the external aim-maker can do is to transmit the symbols in writing or in speech. He cannot directly transmit any aim, for between the mind of the external aim-maker and the act of aiming is the mind of a second person which will choose aim-making before aiming. And it is part of the same distinction between the logic of aim-making and the logic of aiming that no aim-maker can possibly know another's mind so precisely as to have the capacity to prescribe an aim for him that will be perfectly appropriate to his unique mental constitution. When an educationist presumes to have this power, his stance is often remote, pompous, and insensitive, and the gulf between him as aim-maker and the pupil as aimer may widen to such an extent that all possibility of aiming is nullified.

Perhaps the greatest obstacles to clear understanding of educational aims have their common source in the practice of formulating predigested values for others, as personal interests, comprehension, values, and experience may combine to repel them. Conversely, perhaps the clearest perspective on educational aims is from the viewpoint of the learner as a perceiving, value-making subject, free to respond in *his* way, according to his individual nature, rather than to the values of others or the supposedly homogeneous nature of his generalized group. This is not to discredit either the strength of individual-group interaction or the necessary habit-forming influences of teachers and parents on younger children, but merely to reassert the power and uniqueness of personal acceptance and rejection, transcending both speculative generalization and normative impositions.